The Timeless Service of Alpha Kappa Alpha Sorority, Inc.

Small in Numbers, Mighty in Service

UPSILON DELTA OMEGA CHAPTER

AuthorHouse™
1663 Liberty Drive
Bloomington, IN 47403
www.authorhouse.com
Phone: 1-800-839-8640

Published by AuthorHouse 02/17/2015

ISBN: 978-1-4969-3234-1 (sc)
*   978-1-4969-3235-8 (e)*

Library of Congress Control Number: 2014914524

Print information available on the last page.

This book is printed on acid-free paper.

Background Cover Artwork by Theresa Andrews

Contents

Introduction

In the beginning, there was a small group of committed, educated, African-American women; they created Alpha Kappa Alpha Sorority, Incorporated (AKA). I am proud to say that this life-changing event occurred in 1908 at my alma mater, Howard University. More than 85 years later, another small group of committed, educated, African-American women chartered the Upsilon Delta Omega Chapter (UDO). In 2014 we will celebrate 20 years of outstanding service. There have been many books documenting the history of the sorority overall. However, this is the first book ever written to chronicle the history and achievements of this chapter of AKA. The story of the charter members and those who came after them is recorded here within the pages of this book. In addition to the history of UDO, the history of its service and commitment to community are presented in this beautiful expression of sisterhood.

As you read the pages of this book, you will feel the love and commitment of the members come through in everything that we've done. UDO is a small chapter, but as the title of this book suggests, we are, by no means, small in service or impact. In these pages, you will find an active chapter that raises the bar for what can be achieved by dedicated group of women.

Beginning with the South Valley Interest Group, you will see that the chapter's roots are deeply embedded in sisterhood, education, and service to the community. This book introduces you to the five amazing women who made up that group and beautifully displays the projects that were accomplished in their journey to become a new Camden County Chapter, called Upsilon Delta Omega Chapter. The interest group addressed the many needs of the community, which set the stage for the chapter. Once chartered, the chapter was relentless in executing the dynamic program initiatives of the international sorority, as well as its own goals, which are represented in this historical document. This book will allow you the opportunity to experience each member's Alpha Kappa Alpha voice. You will find voices of love, compassion, ingenuity, commitment, high ethical standards, intelligence, elegance, and above all, sisterhood.

As you finish the book you will see how timeless our commitment to service is and why, in 2013, we received a regional award for Overall Outstanding Programs, among other awards previously earned. We have vividly displayed our commitment and love in the pictures, descriptions and summaries within this book. We hope that it will inspire readers to also commit their lives in some way to community service. I invite you to act on that inspiration and prepare to be more fulfilled in life as you do. In the meantime, read this amazing account of a 'small but mighty' group of Alpha Kappa Alpha women and appreciate the blood and sweat that went into creating this piece of chronological art. I proudly and lovingly present to you Upsilon Delta Omega Chapter.

Angela V. Lee
President, UDO
Cherry Hill, New Jersey
January 2014

UPSILON DELTA OMEGA CHAPTER 2013

Greek Officer Names and Titles

The Sorority uses Greek terminology in the identification of its officers and other significant references. The position or title preceded by "Supreme" indicates an International level position. To maximize your reading experience of this book, please review the translations below.

Greek Titles and References	Translations
Basileus	President
1st Anti-Basileus	1st Vice-President
2nd Anti-Basileus	2nd Vice-President
Grammateus	Recording Secretary
Anti- Grammateus	Assistant Secretary
Pecunious Grammateus	Financial Secretary
Tamiouchos	Treasurer
Anti-Tamiouchos	Assistant Treasurer
Epistoleus	Corresponding Secretary
Hodegos	Hostess
Philacter	Sergeant at Arms
Parliamentarian	Parliamentarian
Ivy Leaf Reporter	Publicity Chairman
Historian	Historian
Custodian	Keeper of Records
Chaplain	Chaplain
Soror	Greek for "Sister" used by members
Boule	Governing body – meets biennially
Ivy Beyond the Wall	A Deceased member
Directorate	Board of Directors (Includes Regional)

Acknowledgments

To complete a project of this magnitude takes the commitment and cooperation of a team. This is especially true when the team has very little knowledge about – and no experience with – publishing a book. All we knew was that it had to get done, and if we were going to do it…we were going to do it right! I would like to acknowledge the entire Upsilon Delta Omega chapter for their cooperation, their diligence in submitting information as the committee requested it, and their patience with the committee as we continued to extend our "deadline" dates.

Many thanks go out to the Timeless History Committee and our Editing Committee for maintaining a sisterly attitude throughout this process, for taking on assignments without hesitation, and being willing to meet into the wee hours of the night at times in order to complete this task. Sometimes it felt as though we met for hours and accomplished very little, but alas…we were actually making progress. Patience was the key to our sanity.

We are grateful for all of our families, who have endured our absence from the homefront as we planned and drafted this book. There is a very special "Honey Do" who deserves kudos from this chapter for allowing us to use his office and equipment to hold our regular meetings, organize, scan, and make copies. Yes, we even had him working with us as well. Tony Butler, we will always appreciate your generosity. Martin Allen, you also deserve a gracious "thank you" because without your contribution, we would not have had the beautiful chapter photo for this book, as well as some of our headshots! Both of you "Honey Do's" have made this journey smoother.

We also offer warm thanks to our President, Angela Lee. We did not want to bother you…but we did. Well, you had to approve everything anyway, so why not take a short cut in some areas–especially in graphics – and just let you do it?! Your guidance and expertise were invaluable and we appreciate your thoughtful input.

It was a challenge, but we had fun! The time spent reminiscing as we scanned through pictures, articles, fliers, and the variety of documents which authenticate this chapter's history was priceless.

If there is a lesson gained in every life experience, we can honestly say that in this experience we have learned that regardless of what the mission may be….our Small and Mighty Chapter, Upsilon Delta Omega is up to the task! Thank you all for your cooperation and input.

Gwendolyn Taylor Cobb
Chairman - Timeless History Committee

Timeless History Committee	*Volunteers*	*Editors*
Sheila Weeks Brown	Donna Walker	Angela V. Lee, President
Diane Bruce	Charisse Wheeler	Kamala Allen
Cheryl Butler	Shabett Harper	Tina Browne Sills
Norma Evans	Tina Browne Sills	Allie T. Cobb
Patricia McGhee		

5

Sisterhood

Culture

Victory's Height

We help each other

There's no other

Merit

We strive

Sincere and Rare

Loyal Hearts

ALPHA KAPPA ALPHA SORORITY, INCORPORATED

A Legacy of Sisterhood and Timeless Service

Confined to what she called "a small circumscribed life" in the segregated and male-dominated milieu that characterized the early 1900s, Howard University co-ed Ethel Hedgeman dreamed of creating a support network for women with like minds, coming together for mutual uplift, and coalescing their talents and strengths for the benefit of others. In 1908, her vision crystallized as Alpha Kappa Alpha, the first Negro Greek-letter sorority. Five years later (1913), lead incorporator Nellie Quander ensured Alpha Kappa Alpha's perpetuity through incorporation in the District of Columbia.

Together with eight other coeds at the mecca for Negro education, Hedgeman crafted a design that not only fostered interaction, stimulation, and ethical growth among members; it also provided hope for the masses. From the core group of nine at Howard, AKA has grown into a force of more than 265,000 collegiate members and alumnae, constituting 972 chapters in 42 states, the District of Columbia, the US Virgin Islands, the Bahamas, Germany, South Korea, Japan, Liberia, and Canada.

Because they believed that Negro college women represented "the highest – more education, more enlightenment, and more of almost everything that the great mass of Negroes never had," Hedgeman and her cohorts worked to honor what she called "an everlasting debt to raise them (Negroes) up and to make them better." For more than a century, the Alpha Kappa Alpha Sisterhood has fulfilled that obligation by becoming an indomitable force for good in their communities, state, nation, and the world.

The Alpha Kappa Alpha program today still reflects the communal consciousness steeped in the AKA tradition and embodied in AKA's credo, "To be supreme in service to all mankind." Cultural awareness and social advocacy marked Alpha Kappa Alpha's infancy, but within one year (1914) of acquiring corporate status, AKA had also made its mark on education by establishing a scholarship award. The programming was a prelude to the thousands of pioneering and enduring initiatives that eventually defined the Alpha Kappa Alpha brand.

Through the years, Alpha Kappa Alpha has used the Sisterhood as a grand lever to raise the status of African-Americans, particularly girls and women. AKA has enriched minds and encouraged life-long learning; provided aid for the poor, the sick, and underserved; initiated social action to advance human and civil rights; worked collaboratively with other groups to maximize outreach on progressive endeavors; and continually produced leaders to continue its credo of service.

Guided by twenty-eight international presidents from Nellie M. Quander (1913-1919) to Carolyn House Stewart (2010-2014), with reinforcement from a professional headquarters staff since 1949; AKA's corps of volunteers has instituted groundbreaking social action initiatives and social service programs that have timelessly transformed communities for the better—continually emitting progress in cities, states, the nation, and the world.

Signature Program Initiatives

2000s—Launched Emerging Young Leaders, a bold move to prepare 10,000 girls in grades 6-8 to excel as young leaders equipped to respond to challenges of the 21st century (2011); initiated homage for civil rights milestones by honoring the Little Rock Nine's 1957 desegregation of Central High (Little Rock, Ar.) following the Supreme Court's 1954 decision declaring segregated schools unconstitutional; donated $1 million to Howard University to fund scholarships and preserve Black culture (2008); strengthened the reading skills of 16,000 children through a $1.5 million after-school demonstration project in low-performing, economically deprived, inner city schools (2002); and improved the quality of life for people of African descent through continuation of aid to African countries.

1990s—Built 10 schools in South Africa (1998); added the largest number of minorities to the National Bone Marrow Registry (1996); became first civilian organization to create a memorial to World War II unsung hero Doris (Dorie) Miller (1991).

1980s—Adopted more than 27 African villages, earning Africare's 1986 Distinguished Service Award (1986); encouraged awareness of and participation in the nation's affairs, registering more than 350,000 new voters; and established the Alpha Kappa Alpha Educational Advancement Foundation (1981), a multi-million dollar entity that annually awards more than $100,000 in scholarships, grants, and fellowships.

1970s—Was the only sorority to be named an inaugural member of Operation Big Vote (1979); pledge of one-half million dollars to the United Negro College Fund completed (1976); and purchased Dr. Martin Luther King's boyhood home for the MLK Center for Social Change (1972).

1960s—Sponsored inaugural Domestic Travel Tour, a one-week cultural excursion for 30 high school students (1969); launched a "Heritage Series" on African-American achievers (1965); and emerged as the first women's group to win a grant to operate a federal job corps center (1965), preparing youth 16-21 to function in a highly competitive economy.

1950s—Promoted investing in Black businesses by depositing the initial $38,000 for the AKA Investment Fund with the first and only Negro firm on Wall Street (1958). Spurred Sickle Cell Disease research and education with grants to Howard University Hospital and publication of *The Sickle Cell Story* (1958).

1940s—Invited other Greek-letter organizations to come together to establish the American Council on Human Rights to empower racial uplift and economic development (1948). Acquired observer status from the United Nations (1946); and challenged the absence of people of color from pictorial images used by the government to portray Americans (1944).

1930s—Became first organization to acquire NAACP life membership (1939). Created nation's first Congressional lobby that impacted legislation on issues ranging from decent living conditions and jobs to lynching (1938); and established the nation's first mobile health clinic, providing relief to 15,000 Negroes plagued by famine and disease in the Mississippi Delta (1935).

1920s—Worked to dispel notions that Negroes were unfit for certain professions, and guided Negroes in avoiding career mistakes (1923); pushed anti-lynching legislation (1921).

1900s—Promoted Negro culture and encouraged social action through presentation of Negro artists and social justice advocates, including elocutionist Nathaniel Guy, Hull House founder Jane Addams, and U.S. Congressman Martin Madden (1908-1915). Established the first organizational scholarship at Howard University (1914).

--Earnestine Green McNealey, Ph.D., AKA Historian
August 2013

The Notable North Atlantic Region

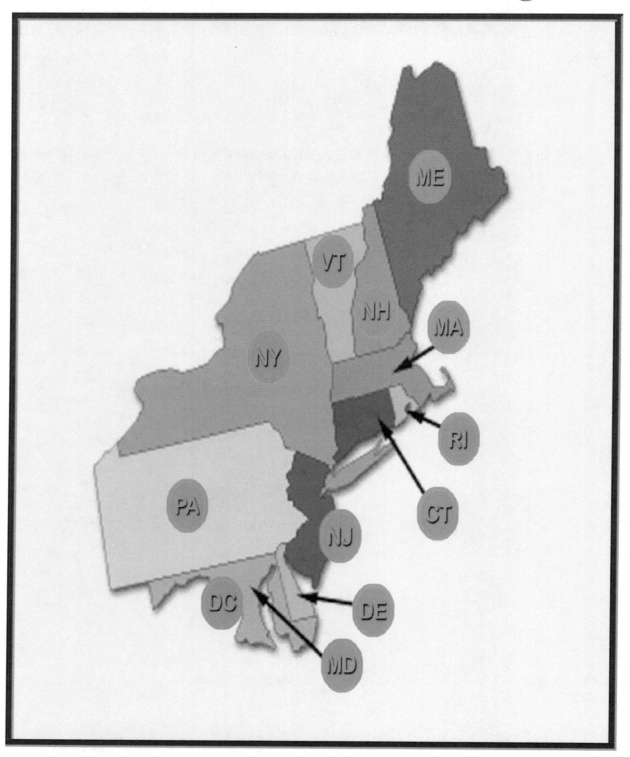

ALPHA KAPPA ALPHA SORORITY, INCORPORATED
NORTH ATLANTIC REGION
A Legacy of Sisterhood and Timeless Service

The history of the North Atlantic Region of Alpha Kappa Alpha Sorority, Incorporated is deeply embedded in the northeastern region of the United States. Extending from New England to the District of Columbia, the North Atlantic Region is the birthplace of the Sorority, which occurred at the cradle of higher education for African Americans on the campus of Howard University in Washington, D.C.

It was during rapidly changing social and economic conditions in America that a group of young Howard women under the guidance of a visionary, Ethel Hedgeman (Lyle), decided to assume leadership roles in sisterhood and service to the community. The creation of Alpha Kappa Alpha in 1908 symbolized a desire to shape not only their own destiny, but countless others' as well.

History reveals the success of Nellie Quander's efforts to ensure the perpetuity of Alpha Kappa Alpha; incorporation was ultimately secured in the District of Columbia in 1913, with Alpha Chapter at Howard University as the first chapter. Quander, who became the first AKA international president, was instrumental in the development of the Alpha Kappa Alpha Endowed Scholarship at Howard University in 1914.

Ten years after incorporation, the Sorority established a national presence with chapters and members from the Atlantic to the Pacific Coast. Historically, as the sorority grew and developed, it established Regional entities. The first seven regions were approved in 1925. The North Atlantic Region covers the following states: Connecticut, Delaware, District of Columbia, Eastern New York, Eastern Pennsylvania, Maine, Maryland, Massachusetts, New Hampshire, New Jersey, Rhode Island and Vermont. The growth of college and alumnae members has allowed the reach of Alpha Kappa Alpha to expand across the United States, the District of Columbia, the Virgin Islands and internationally.

As Alpha Kappa Alpha's second-largest region, North Atlantic's rich history is interwoven in the leadership and programs of the 32 women who have served with distinction as Regional Organizers and Directors:

Nellie Quander	Mary C. Wright Thompson	Mildred Stuart
Grace Hill Jacobs	Ruth A. Scott	Nellie Wolfe Gaylord
Vivian Carter Mason	Leatha Hermanchandra	Ruth Coles Easley
Erma Bruce Davis	Sophie Fowler	Idell S. Pugh
Portia Wiley Nickens	Lillian M. Parrott Murphy	Erma W. Barron
Norma E. Boyd	Marjorie Holloman Parker	Wilma Holmes Tootle
Viola Lewis	Emma Bell Brinkley	C. Edith Booker
Erma Bruce Davis	Emma G. Bright	Joy Elaine Daley
Thelma Berlack Boozier	Aloncita J. Flood	Evelyn Sample-Oates
Edna Over Gray Campbell	Esther Garland Pollard	Constance R. Pizarro
Sadie St. Clair	Anne Mitchem Davis	

Leadership in greater service to Alpha Kappa Alpha has been the region's hallmark since its inception. Starting with Nellie Quander, five International Presidents have come from the North Atlantic Region, including B. Beatrix Scott, Dorothy B. Ferebee, Edna Over Gray Campbell and Marjorie Holloman Parker.

A Notable Legacy

The North Atlantic Region was branded the "Notable North Atlantic" in 1994 by 28th Regional Director Wilma Holmes Tootle due to its outstanding accomplishments and distinction as the genesis of Alpha Kappa Alpha and home of six founders. The region is also the site of the sorority's incorporation, the birthplace of the first International President, home of the composer of the National Hymn, the designer of the Founders' Memorial Window as well as a past Ivy Leaf editor. In addition, the Alpha Kappa Alpha international repository is housed at the Moorland-Spingarn Research Center at Howard University, which is also home to the Founders' Memorial Window at Andrew Rankin Memorial Chapel.

The sorority held its first Boule in Washington, DC in December 1918. Fourteen Boules have been hosted in the region, including the milestone Golden, Diamond and Centennial anniversary celebrations.

From a programmatic perspective, the region's 71 graduate chapters and 65 undergraduate chapters have focused on various initiatives, including health, education, civil rights, the arts and technology, as part of the sorority's more than 265,000 members in 972 chapters worldwide. Since the mid-1980s, the chapters of the region have grouped into five clusters, a concept that has further enhanced the strong link of sisterhood shared by all Alpha Kappa Alpha women. The first Cluster Leadership Conference was held in 1987.

The region's history has been consistently recorded since the 1950s, beginning with The History of Alpha Kappa Alpha Sorority in the North Atlantic Region 1908-1952 written by Ruth B. Josephs. In 1986, Ruth C. Easley updated the history with the publication of The North Atlantic Story Since 1952. Wilma Holmes Tootle took up the charge to continue telling the North Atlantic story with the publication of North Atlantic Regional History 1986-1998. With the appointment of Janette Hoston Harris as the first Regional Historian in 2008, the fourth regional history – A History of Sisterhood and Service…The Legacy Continues – was prepared for the sorority's Centennial. This marked the first comprehensive publication of chapter histories, charterings, clusters and regional directors, and was followed by a regional pocket directory in 2010.

The international histories of Alpha Kappa Alpha have captured the origins, growth and accomplishments of the North Atlantic Region, including In the Eye of the Beholder and Past is Prologue by Marjorie Parker, and Earnestine Green McNealey's Pearls of Service (2006). A century of history and service, bequeathed by the founders, continues to evolve as exemplified in theme of "Global Leadership Through Timeless Service" heralded by 28th International President Carolyn House Stewart. As keeper of the Alpha Kappa Alpha flame, the North Atlantic Region will continue to reign "supreme in service to all mankind."

—Janette Hoston Harris, Ph.D., North Atlantic Regional Historian
September 2013

The South Valley Interest Group

The early 1990s was a period of great change within the United States of America. While several notable events occurred during this era, a few of the most impactful include the Los Angeles Riots, the confirmation of Supreme Court Justice Clarence Thomas, and the first Persian Gulf War. In addition to these significant cultural developments, the typical American household was significantly affected by the national economic recession of the time. It was during this period of noteworthy events that five energetic and determined women began to pursue their common vision of extending the reach of Alpha Kappa Alpha Sorority, Incorporated®. Their purpose was to become a chartered chapter, keeping with the sorority's national guidelines, in order to implement activities that would broaden the service base of Alpha Kappa Alpha within their community.

In 1991, five graduate sorors – Marcia Ashhurst-Whiting, Edith Bennett, Jean Milam, Faye Tucker and Betty Wilson – embarked upon the ultimate objective of their mission: establishing a new chapter through which inactive sorors could once again join the ranks of sisterhood. The question that they pondered was, "How could they appeal to the woman of the 90's, the woman of the 21st century, the secure and dynamic women of Alpha Kappa Alpha Sorority"? These sorors soon realized that the answer already resided within each of them. Each of these women possessed the same values of self-worth, sisterhood, cohesiveness, and service to the community. As they began their journey of recruiting and reclaiming sorors, they continually stressed these traits. Their mission was to engage progressive African-American women who desired to recommit their time, talent, and treasures to Alpha Kappa Alpha within their community.

Soon their numbers began to increase as additional sorors also expressed an interest and a commitment to return to the sisterhood. Their reach extended to twenty-four of Alpha Kappa Alpha's finest women and thus began the South Valley Interest Group. These twenty-four women included Marcia Ashurst-Whiting, Sarah Banks, Edith Bennett, Diane Bruce, Cheryl Butler, Loren Gaffin, Debbie Jenkins, Harriet Jones, Rhonda Jordan, Bettye McCant, Patricia McGhee, Jean R. Milam, Jan Puig, Iris Romantini, LaTanya Taylor, Mary Ellen Tillmon, Faye Tucker, Maria Tucker, Myra Ward, Bonnie Weaver-Niles, Bonne F. Williams, Karen Williams, Betty J. Wilson and Christine Younger. The South Valley Interest Group elected officers in order to provide a collective sense of direction. Soror Erma Barron, the 27th North Atlantic Regional Director, contributed guidance, direction, expertise, and sisterly support to the group throughout its journey toward becoming a chapter. Over the next three years, the group of sorors continued to bond while organizing social events and participating in community service projects that were in line with the sorority's international programs.

The 23rd International President, Mary Shy Scott, endorsed World Community, Education, Family, Health, Economics and The Arts as her signature programs. Under the guidance of Erma Barron, the South Valley Interest Group set up a calendar of events with activities in keeping with the international signature programs. They adopted the Red Oak Manor Nursing Home and donated toiletries and baked goods, read poetry, sang songs and wrote letters. They also donated school supplies to at-risk teenagers in Camden, New Jersey, and they supported the Mister & Miss Teenage World Pageant by purchasing an ad. The group co-sponsored a health fair with local physicians, nurses and other healthcare professionals for an underserved community. To raise money for scholarships, the South Valley Interest Group held its first "Yuletide Jazz Brunch and African-American Art Exhibit" in December 1993; this Christmas gala provided funding for two scholarships and was such a huge success that they decided to make it an annual event, that continues to this day.

The members of the South Valley Interest Group demonstrated that there were unmet needs in their local community – needs that they were willing and able to address. The programs they conceived and executed as an interest group were only a foreshadowing of what they – and those who would later join them – could do as a chapter of Alpha Kappa Alpha Sorority in the South Jersey area.

South Valley Interest Group
1992 - 1994

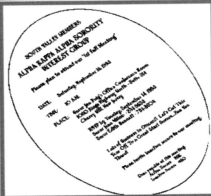

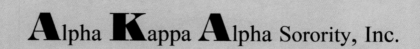

Alpha **K**appa **A**lpha Sorority, Inc.

Upsilon Delta Omega
Chartered June 18, 1994
Voorhees, New Jersey

Friends by Chance
Sisters by Choice

At the one year anniversary of the chapter chartering Soror
Bonnie Weaver-Niles wrote a poem which chronicles the
early history of the Upsilon Delta Omega Chapter.

"Putting it Together"

On January 15, nineteen hundred and eight
Ethel Hedgeman Lyle sought her destiny and fate.
She was the founder of Alpha Kappa Alpha you see,
On Howard University's campus, AKA came to be.

Built on a dream of service to all mankind,
Our founders, women of vision, were a rare find.
Throughout its years, AKA has attracted the very best,
No wonder a small group in South Jersey challenged the test,

Of establishing an Alpha Kappa Alpha chapter in their neighborhood,
Bringing women together, for AKA, could only be good,
So Faye, Betty, Edith, Marsha and Jean
Embarked upon the task of capturing their dream.

On March 11, 1991, the first official meeting was held,
Of the South Valley Interest Group, "Does the name ring a bell?"
They searched South Jersey both near and a far,
For inactive Sorors they might as well have been reaching for the nearest star.

But perseverance and networking soon found their place,
By 1992, Diane, Iris, Cheryl, Chris had been added, "Thanks to God's grace"
Jan and LaTanya also had come aboard,
Their dream, a little closer maybe not impossible …Praise the Lord!

By 1993 and 1994, some more Sorors had come their way,
Debbie, Maria, Rhonda, Bonnie Williams signed up "Making their Day'
(Sarah, Harriet, MaryEllen, Loren, Pat, Karen, Myra, Bonnie Niles)
At last. Oh! At last, the required number of Sorors had been met,
Now the paperwork processing for chaptership, not easy…you can bet.

Applying for chapter status took time and was no fun.
But the group pulled together because the job had to be done.
A meeting in Atlantic City, held the group's fate,

Suddenly, the group began to look like a Chapter-To- Be,
Program activities, fundraisers were planned most carefully.
Red Oak Nursing Home, Christmas gifts for special youth,
Night meetings, healthy disagreements, part of "Putting It Together"
Girl! Ain't that the Truth?

Fundraising activities resulted in setting the pace,
Our two Jazz Brunches were done in style and taste.
Both were successful and when all expenses were paid,
Two young ladies were awarded scholarships for their own future plans to be laid.

Regional meetings were attended by "The Sleepy Six and Styling Four"
Finally… The Big Moment… June 18, Nineteen hundred and ninety four.
The "Vision Had Been Captured"… What more to say?
UPSILON DELTA OMEGA made their debut…Gosh!…"What a Day!"

1995…Began just Great!
More Sorors came aboard bringing their special gifts to our plate.
Shabett, Gwen, Karen, Cassandra signed up you see,
UPSILON DELTA OMEGA… On the move …Growing in maturity.

But, all is not finished: the work has begun,
That is why a piece of this puzzle still remains undone.
It is for all Sorors… Both old and new,
We are hoping UPSILON DELTA OMEGA will be for you.

UPSILON DELTA OMEGA

Charter Members 1994

Upsilon Delta Omega Historical Overview

After three years functioning as the South Valley Interest Group, this enterprising community of Alpha Kappa Alpha women was honored to see their group assume the status of a full-fledged chapter. On Sunday, June 17, 1994, Soror Erma Barron met with the members of the South Valley Interest Group to begin preparation for the chartering ceremony and activities. This represented their last meeting as the South Valley Interest Group. On June 18, 1994, the group was formally presented as Upsilon Delta Omega Chapter, Alpha Kappa Alpha Sorority, Incorporated. Nellie W. Gaylord, the 24th North Atlantic Regional Director and Representative of the International Membership Committee, and Erma Barron, the 27th North Atlantic Regional Director, presided over this inaugural event at The Mansion in Voorhees, New Jersey.

After the chartering ceremony, the chapter's first officers were presented and they were as follows: Jean Milam, Basileus; Faye Tucker, First Anti-Basileus; Betty J. Wilson, Second Anti-Basileus; Cheryl Butler, Grammateus; LaTanya Taylor, Ant-Grammateus; Harriet Jones, Epistoleus; Iris Romantini, Hodegos; Marcia Ashurst-Whiting, Pecunious Grammateus; Edith Bennett, Tamiouchous; Gwen Dancy-Coats, Philacter; Loren Gaffin, Ivy Leag Reporter; Debbie Jenkins, Historian-Archivist; Mary Ellen Tillmon, Custodian-Keeper of Records; Karen Williams, Parliamentarian; and Bonnie Williams, Chaplain.

Since that glorious day of chartering nineteen years ago, the chapter has conducted four Membership Intake Processes, extending membership to other women committed to service to all mankind. These included the "First and Foremost 15" in the spring of 1996 and the "Tenacious Three" in the spring of 2003. Another six members were welcomed into the sisterhood in 2008, and most recently, six ladies of distinction were initiated into the chapter in 2013. Women from each of these groups continue to serve with commitment and contribute their time and talent to increase the chapter's impact on the community.

On June 10, 1996, Upsilon Delta Omega Chapter established its tax-exempt charitable foundation, Sisters That Are Rendering Service, or S.T.A.R.S. The mission of the foundation is to support scholarships and community service projects. This foundation also provides a vehicle for tax-exempt donations, contributions and grants from the community – along with other organizations – to support these efforts.

Today, the Upsilon Delta Omega Chapter continues to expand its presence in the community. Service projects completed during the early years focused on issues such as: the black family, reading and math programs, and health and education for women and children. Some of the early service projects included:

- Participation in the South Jersey Medical Association Community Health Fairs

- Participation in career fairs sponsored by the African Male Institute

- Sponsorship of the Ivy AKAdemy Program and IMAGES Program

- Sponsorship of the First Responders Program

- Sponsorship of Junior/Senior High school students in the AKA-PIMS Program

- Donation of Mother's and Father's Day Baskets that provided food and household items to needy families

- Sponsorship of various activities for the residents of the Anna M. Sample Shelter for Women and Families

- Sponsorship of an Annual AKA Children's Closet that provided donated clothing and school supplies for children

- Sponsorship of the Salute to African-American Men, which honors men who have made significant contributions to the African American community. Past honorees include Johnnie Cochran, Attorney; and Jerry C. Johnson, MD, the first African-American President of the American Geriatric Society

- Sponsorship of the Top of the Game: Reading Programs and workshops on Public Speaking

- Sponsorship of the Annual Yuletide Jazz Brunch, which is UDO's major fundraising event to provide scholarships to three senior female high school students and one male student enrolled in a four year university. To date we have awarded over 75K in scholarships

Upsilon Delta Omega Chapter's more recent work from 2007 through 2013 has focused on issues related to social justice, human rights, health, poverty, economic security and environmental sustainability. The chapter has and continues to address these through the following ongoing service projects:

- Non-Traditional Entrepreneur
    - Economic Smart Fair – From Chaos to Clarity
    - Minority Entrepreneur Networking (AKArd Exchange)

- International Women's Day Event
    - Viewing of "Half the Sky Live"
    - Participating in "Make A Powerful Noise Live"

- Emerging Young Leaders (EYL) Initiative:
    - Youth Finance Educational Workshop
    - Ice Cream Social
    - MLK Day Community Service and Workshops

- Etiquette Seminar

    o   Formal Dining Etiquette

    o   Presentation of Etiquette Book

    o   Dinner at upscale minority-owned restaurant to display etiquette skills

- Health Initiative

    o   American Cancer Society

    o   Making Strides Against Breast Cancer

    o   Heart Health Month at the Good Counsel Home for Unwed Mothers

    o   Pink Goes Red at Blue2o Restaurant

    o   Take a Loved One to the Doctor's event in Philadelphia

    o   Cancer Awareness Workshops

- Global Poverty Initiative

    o   Family Fun Day at the Anna M. Sample Homeless Shelter

    o   Adopt-A-Family Program Holiday Donations

    o   Scholarships for College Bound Students

- Economic Security Initiative

    o   Awarding of four academic scholarships at Scholarship Luncheon

    o   Youth Financial Education Workshops

    o   Adult Financial Education Workshops

- Social Justice and Human Rights Initiative

    o   Voter Registration Drives

    o   UDO attends AKA State House Day in Trenton, NJ

    o   Domestic Violence Workshops

    o   Workshops / Donations – Good Counsel Home for Unwed Mothers

- Internal Leadership Training for External Service Initiative

    o Boule' Attendance

    o North Atlantic Regional Conference

    o Cluster Conferences and Leadership Conferences

    o Leadership Development Webinars

    o Anne Mitchem-Davis Officer's Institute

Upsilon Delta Omega Chapter, "Small in Numbers, Big in Service" received the Overall Outstanding Program Award at the North Atlantic Regional Conference held in Philadelphia, PA, in 2013. The award was recognition of the commitment the chapter has made to implement meaningful service projects under all of the International Program Initiatives.

Chapter Presidents

and

Administrations

Jean Stewart Milam

Born

April 4 – Texas

Primary Vocation

Public School Principal

Education

BA, Prairie View A &M University
EdD, University of Pennsylvania

Major Imprint in Office

- Led the chapter in the implementation of the Images Program through the IVY AKAdemy and in preparing students to participate in the PIMS Program

- Led the chapter in the Red Oaks Nursing Home Adopt-a-Senior Program

- Oversaw the chapter's participation in the South Jersey Medical Association Heath Fair

- Initiated chapter's participation in the Black College Fair

- Spearheaded chapter members' collection of clothing items that were donated to the New Jersey Youth Program

- Led chapter members in the First and Second Salute to African-American Men

- Oversaw chapter participation in a radio-thon to raise money for a local adoption agency

- Led the chapter in the collection of school supplies for students in African countries

- Oversaw the chapter's implementation of the annual Yuletide Jazz Brunch held each December as the chapter's major scholarship fundraiser

Alpha Kappa Alpha Lineage

Initiated: Theta Pi Omega Chapter, 1978

South Valley Interest Group
President, 1992-1994

Upsilon Delta Omega Chapter
First Basileus, 1994-1999

Chapter Officers

Basileus - Jean Milam
First Anti-Basileus - Faye Tucker
Second Anti-Basileus - Iris Romantini
Grammateus - Cheryl Butler
Anti-Grammateus - LaTanya Taylor
Pecunious Grammateus - Marcia Ashurst-Whiting
Epistoleus - Rhonda Jordan
Tamiouchos - Edith Bennett
Hodegos - Bonnie Weaver-Niles
Philacter - Gwen Dancy-Coats
Ivy Leaf Reporter - Loren Gaffin
Historian - Diane Bruce
Custodian/Keeper of Records - Mary Ellen Tillmon

Chapter Members

Kamala Allen
Trudi Alston
Caren Ashmon
Sarah Banks
Tonya Barge
Yvonne Tracie Boatwright
Lori Brown-Sharpe
Ernestine Buck
Clara Henderson
Debbie Jenkins
Harriett Jones
Monika Jones
Diane Kirkpatrick
Sherry Ellis Knight
Donna Lane
Denise Mason
Shaun Mason
Bettye McCant

Patricia McGhee
Lisa Morrison
Tanya Nelson-Rice
Frances Paul
Tamika Paul
Gloria Pierce
Cassandra Poe-Johnson
Jan Puig
Wendy Scales-Johnson
Tina Browne Sills
Carole Sims-Austin
Maria Tucker
Myra Ward
Bonnie Williams
Karen Williams
Betty Wilson
Christine Younger

Highlights of Soror Jean Milam
First Upsilon Delta Omega Basileus

Upsilon Delta Omega Chartered in North Atlantic Region

Voorhees, N. J. – Twenty-four noted became charter members of Upsilon Delta Omega Chapter on June 18, 1994. The ceremony was officiated by Soror Freda H. Barron, former North Atlantic regional director, Soror Hattie Gaylord, North Atlantic regional representative, International Membership Committee, assisted with the ceremony. The charter chapter members are Marcia Barbara Whiting, Sandi Stephs, Edith Bennett, Ilene Bruce, Cheryl Urias, Susan J. Cahin, Debbie Amboy, Norma Jones, Rhonda Jordan, Bettye McCant, Juanita McPhaid, Jean ...

... H. Milam, Jan Hook, Iris Honeworth, LaTonya Taylor, Mary Ellen Yelpman, Faye Tucker, Rhea Tucker, Myra Ware, Bonnie Wassam-Nibbs, Majorie Williams, Karen Withers, Betty J. Wilson, and Christine Younger.

The ceremony was followed by a reception for visiting sorors, a champagne toast, and a public luncheon attended by the community members, Milam Chapter members, families and friends. The proceeds from this affair will be used to establish a scholarship fund for graduates and for her involvement in community activities. Upsilon Delta Omega celebrated her chartering and sisterhood with a twilight picnic held at the home of Soror Edith Bennett.

The luncheon, planned to present and celebrate a new graduate chapter of 24 women in the South Jersey area, was presided over by charter member Sarah Banks.

... potatoes, rolls and butter, coffee and tea, were Alberta Wright, Gloria Pierce, Pamela L. Mitchell, Denise Green, Alyce Thomas, Maxine Evers and Felicia Stokes.

Family members, friends and ... Jackson, Dorothy Collins, Fraul Cyrus, Rose Cruz, Mary Brown Clara Henderson, Veronica Storks, Randy Landis, Celeste Robinson, Dora Ruller and Lovey Mitchell.

Sharing "tid-bits" as they enjoyed the white chocolate marquis dessert were Bonnie Knight, Celeste Robinson, Alyce Thomas, Anne Guither, Jeanne Holmes, Marie Akins, Gloria Gibson, Edith Bennett, Melvia Scott, Alease Scott, John and Mary Holt, Vauetta Kersey, Anita McLaurin, Linda Sykes, Randy Landis, Dawn McLaurin, Carolyn Henderson, Angela Renee Puia, George McLaurin and many ...

IMAGES teaches about etiquette as well as how to interview for colleges and jobs.

Alpha Kappa Alpha Sorority, Inc.
Upsilon Delta Omega Chapter

Presents its
Second Annual Scholarship
"Yuletide Jazz Brunch"

Sunday, December 18, 1994
1 P.M. - 5 P.M.
Auletto's Catering
Almonesson, New Jersey

Voorhees, NJ

Upsilon Delta Omega Launches IMAGES Program

Upsilon Delta Omega Chapter successfully completed its first AKAdemy program, IMAGES (Identity, Mastery, Achievement, Goals, Enrichment = Success). The chapter cosponsored this program with the borough of Chesilhurst, N.J.

The program provided an extensive five-month schedule of workshops to thirty girls, ages 12 ... posed an IMAGES II program. A reception followed the ceremony.

Voorhees, NJ

Upsilon Delta Omega Salutes African-American Men

Upsilon Delta Omega Chapter honored 13 African-American men who have made and continue to make contributions to the community. The men and the categories in which they were honored were the following: State Senator Wayne R. Bryant (politics); Deputy Imperial Potentate for Prince ...

For black girls, lessons in success come from a sorority program

By Brian Thevenot
STAFF WRITER

CHESILHURST — Watch the legal coverage on CNN about a decade from now, and you might just see Mike Highsmith ...

... between 12 and 18 years old.

IMAGES (Identity, Mastery, Achievement, Goals, Enrichment, Success) is designed and run locally, but is part of AKA's Ivy AKAdemy initiative, which seeks to pro- ...

... his mother. "They're interested in developing the whole person, and I think that it is very unique. My daughters have been in programs that target the community, or one community project or another. But ...

T. Faye Tucker

Born

September 18 - Richmond, Virginia

Primary Vocation

Retired Educator - Business Teacher

Education

BA, Education, Temple University

Major Imprint in Office

- Led the chapter with the implementation of all national programs which included the Black Family; The Ivy AKAdemy program which was co-sponsored with the Borough of Chesilhurst, and the "On Track" tutoring program.

- Oversaw the chapter's commitment to community outreach through such activities as AKA Coat Day, Black Dollar Month and the Special Olympics Summer Games.

- Continued the chapter's signature program – Salute to African-American Men.

- Yuletide Jazz Brunch

Alpha Kappa Alpha Lineage

Initiated: Delta Mu Chapter
Temple University, Philadelphia, PA

South Valley Interest Group, 1993

Upsilon Delta Omega Chapter
Charter Member, 1994

Offices Held: First Anti-Basileus

Chapter Officers

Basileus - T. Faye Tucker
Anti-Basileus - Dr. Sarah Banks, Norma R. Evans
Grammateus - Shabett Harper
Anti-Grammateus - Sherry Ellis Knight
Pecunious Grammateus - Bonnie Williams
Anti-Pecunious Grammateus - Betty Jane Wilson
Tamiouchos - Patricia McGhee
Epistoleus - Monika Jones, Debbie Jenkins
Hodegos - Yvonne Tracie Boatwright
Parliamentarian - Karen McGlashan Williams
Ivy Leaf Reporter - Donna Lane
Historian - Carole Sims-Austin
Philacter - Cheryl Butler
Chaplain - Betty Jane Wilson, Mary Ellen Tillmon

Chapter Members

Kamala D. Allen
Trudi G. Alston
Caren Ashmon
Edith Bennett
Ernestine Buck
Lori Brown-Sharpe
Bridgette Crafton
Loren Gaffin
Clara Henderson
Harriet Jones

Jerri Kendrick
Diane Kirkpatrick
Lisa M. Morrison
Tanya Nelson-Rice
Gloria Pierce
Cassandra Poe-Johnson
Tina Browne Sills
Jean R. Stewart
Maria Tucker
Christine Lee Younger

Highlights of Soror T. Faye Tucker
Second Upsilon Delta Omega Basileus

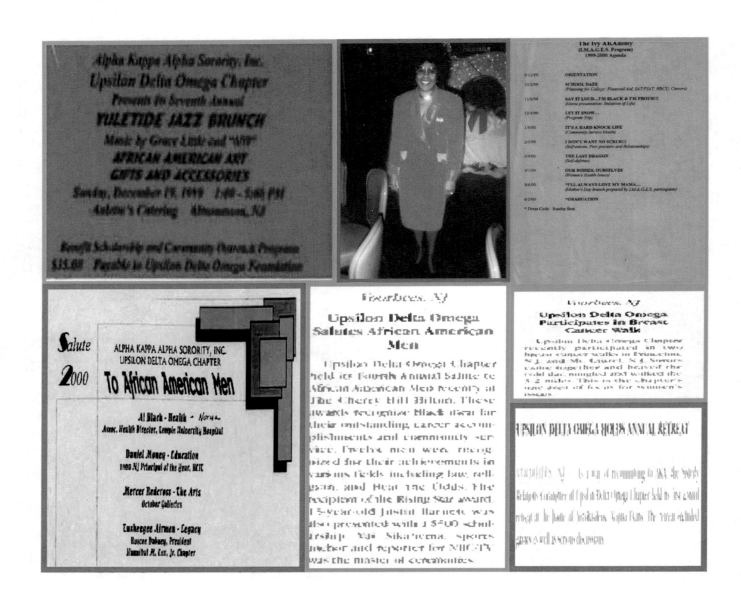

Norma R. Evans, Esquire

Born

June 15 – Washington, D.C.

Primary Vocation

Deputy Attorney General
New Jersey Office of the Attorney General

Education

BS, Communications, Towson University
Juris Doctor, Temple University
School of Law

Alpha Kappa Alpha Lineage

Initiated: Lambda Beta Chapter
Townson University-1978

Upsilon Delta Omega, 1997-Present

Offices Held: Ivy Leaf Reporter,
Parliamentarian, First Anti-Basileus,
Basileus

Regional Appointments:
Regional Protocol Committee Member

Chairman, North Atlantic Region Centennial
Luncheon Committee "AKA Favorite Things"

Co-Chairman, North Atlantic Regional
Conference – 2011

Cluster IV Rep to the Regional Program
Committee
Publicity Committee – NARC 2010
Transportation Committee – NARC 2005
NARC Workshop Facilitator
Regional Conference Choir Member

Major Imprint in Office

- Coined the phrase "Small in Numbers, Mighty in Service" as the chapter motto
- First Basileus to lead the chapter to Regional Awards - Small Chapter of the Year and Outstanding Exhibit Award
- Implemented Buckle Up Seatbelt Safety program and Poster Contest at East Camden Middle School, Camden, NJ
- Expanded AKA Coat Day by collaborating with retailers to offer vouchers for the purchase of a new coat
- Collaborated with local Fire Departments to donate smoke detectors under the AKAlarm initiative

Chapter Officers

Basileus - Norma R. Evans
First Anti-Basileus - Bridgette Crafton, Lisa Goodman, Patricia McGhee
Second Anti-Basileus - Kamala D. Allen
Grammateus - Lisa Goodman
Pecunious Grammateus - Betty Jane Wilson
Tamiouchos - Bonnie Williams, Brenda Dailey-Holmes
Epistoleus - Lisa Goodman, Angela Lee
Ivy Leaf Reporter - Gwendolyn Cobb
Parliamentarian - Karen McGlashan Williams
Hodegos - Shabett Harper
Philacter - Cheryl Butler
Historian - Carole Sims-Austin, Yvonne Tracie Boatwright
Chaplain - Mary Ellen Tillmon

Chapter Members

Cheryl Butler
Erica Henderson
Danielle Jean-Pierre
Sherry Knight
Alanda M. Koon
Amanda M. Koon
Cassandra Poe-Johnson

Linda Robinson
Lori Brown-Sharpe
Tina Browne Sills
Carole Sims-Austin
Donna Thomas
LaSandra Watkins
Sheila Weeks Brown

Highlights of Soror Norma Evans
Third Upsilon Delta Omega Basileus

Upsilon Delta Omega Salutes African American Men

Upsilon Delta Omega salutes African American men

RHEES, NJ — Upsilon Delta Omega Chapter presented its sixth S African American Men. The award ceremony recognizes Af erican men for their outstanding career accomplishments vice to their communities. Among this year's recipients were Be pkins, WBA, WBO & IBF Middleweight Champion; John Blunt, AU, Channel 10 Anchor; Dr. Jerry Johnson, the first African Ame

Upsilon Delta Omega Launches Pilot Reading Program

CHERRY HILL, NJ — Upsilon Delta Omega Chapter launched its Ivy Reading AKAdemy Pilot Program this past summer at two local elementary schools. The goal of the Ivy Reading AKAdemy is to give students the reading time, support and guidance that is necessary to enable them to read at or above grade level by the time they complete the primary grades. This reading initiative focuses on early learning and mastery of basic reading skills by the end of the third grade. In alliance with the national initiative, Upsilon Delta Omega Chapter has donated a set of five books per child for a third

Upsilon Delta Omega Salutes African-American Men

CHERRY HILL, NJ — Upsilon Delta Omega Chapter hosted it's seventh "Salute to African-American Men." The purpose of the salute is to honor African-American men and enrich, empower and enlighten those within the communities in which they live. The salute provides a medium to show appreciation for the accomplishments of those exceptional African-American men for their service, dedication and commitment to their families and communities. These men have gone beyond the call of duty to make a difference. This year, Upsilon Delta Omega honored individuals in eight categories. Those categories included sports, health, media,

Upsilon Delta Omega's Aids Injured Rising Star

Voorhees, New Jersey - Rising Star Recipient for the 2000 Salute to African American Men, Adam Taliaferro was injured during a Penn State football game during his starting season as a freshman. Adam was selected as the Rising Star because he demonstrated strong scholastic abilities as well as excelled in

Upsilon Delta Omega Hosts 11th Annual Yuletide Jazz Brunch

CHERRY HILL, NJ — Upsilon Delta Omega Chapter held its annual Jazz Brunch. This is one of the chapter's signature events and each year becomes more popular in the community. Under the leadership of Soror Patricia McGhee, Jazz Brunch chairman, chapter members were enthusiastic and aggressive in promoting the event, which raised the attendance this year to approximately 300 guests. Sorors and guests enjoyed an afternoon in an elegant setting that included a jazz band that performed many popular tunes for relaxing and dancing. There were a variety of delicious foods and countless door prizes and giveaways. Also included in the festivities were vendors with unique items for sale. Over the years, this event has proven to be Upsilon Delta Omega's most successful fund-raiser. The majority of the money raised during this event continues to provide scholarships to many high school seniors throughout the area.

Upsilon Delta Omega Sponsors AKA Children's Closet

The committee chairman, Soror Betty Wilson, looks on as a young boy smiles with satisfaction as he holds his newly acquired roller blades.

CHERRY HILL, NJ — Upsilon Delta Omega Chapter, in collaboration with the Woodland Avenue Presbyterian Church of Camden, N.J., sponsored the first annual AKA Children's Closet. The purpose of the children's closet is to provide free clothing to those in need. Sorors gathered clothes from several sources and spent many hours sorting by size and gender to organize for this event. There were coats and a variety of clothing of all types. The sizes ranged from infant to children's size 16. Reverend Floyd L. White, III, Pastor of Woodland Presbyterian Church, provided a continental breakfast for sorors. A youth group from the church participated by preparing and serving lunch to sorors and those church members who assisted in setting up and manning the tables of clothing. An artist did face painting for the children and a registered nurse volunteered her time to take blood pressure for adults.

The Timeless Service of Upsilon Delta Omega Chapter

Norma R. Evans, Esquire

2001 - 2004

Upsilon Delta Omega Chapter's third Basileus was a member of the chapter for fewer than four years when she ascended to the position. Norma became the Basileus during a difficult time in the chapter's history with no prior UDO Basilei remaining. Consequently, she had the monumental task of rebuilding the chapter, while executing the initiatives set forth by the administrations of Supreme Basilei, Norma Solomon White and Linda Marie White.

Upon her election to the position of Basileus, Norma pledged to be a servant leader. As such, she would be the first to roll up her sleeves and do whatever work needed to be done to accomplish the goal. With as few as 17 members, Norma led the chapter in outstanding community service events. Most notably was the chapter's annual execution of the "AKA Children's Closet," which provided clothing and school supplies to children in one of the nation's most impoverished communities, Camden, NJ. Under Norma's leadership, with the fewest members in the history of the chapter. UDO gained regional recognition for its outstanding service projects for the first time.

During her tenure, Norma single-handedly compiled the first award-winning submission for the Regional Award of Small Chapter of the Year. However, she always recognized that the chapter could not have received such an honor without its dedicated members. She acknowledged the talents of all. Ultimately, she received the "UDO Sisterliness Award" for setting a living example to the membership.

"Everybody's life is a warning or an example. You've got to decide what you're going to be and you have to draw a line in the sand."

One of her most memorable moments as Basileus was when she had the privilege of participating in the initiation ceremony of Honorary Member, Alicia Keys. Norma went on to serve the sorority as the Chairman of the notable North Atlantic Region's Centennial Luncheon in 2008. "AKA Favorite Things" was a spectacular event, where members received luxury pink and green gifts. She was also selected to co-chair the North Atlantic Regional Conference in 2011.

Norma is married to Calvin Evans and they have two children, Kirstin Evans – also a member of Alpha Kappa Alpha, and Calvin Evans, Jr., better known to all as "CJ."

Patricia Yvonne McGhee

Major Imprint in Office

- Increased scholarship awards from three to four
- Began collaborative efforts with two other local chapters in the area of Voter Registration
- Led chapter in collaboration with Pi Mu Omega and Theta Pi Omega to begin an economic literacy campaign
- Led chapter in hosting the Cluster IV Conference in 2006
- Co-Chaired Transportation Committee for 2005 NARC
- Led the chapter in growth from 22 members to 37 members
- Led chapter in implementing the Ivy Reading AKAdemy at an elementary school in Burlington, NJ
- Led chapter implementation of the First Responders Program at a high school in Winslow Township, NJ
- Led chapter in participation in the Young Authors Program in which our entrant, China Owens from East Camden Middle School, won honorable mention for her story and was published in the Young Authors North Atlantic Regional publication
- Strengthened chapter's support of the Black Family through efforts at major holidays and adoption of a Family Homeless Shelter in Camden, NJ
- Led chapter through a successful Alpha Kappa Alpha Sorority, Inc., chapter evaluation

Born

April 12 – Camden, New Jersey

Primary Vocation

Retired Educator – Media Specialist, Camden County Public Schools

Education

BA, English, Rutgers University, Camden, New Jersey
MA, School and Public Librarianship, Rowan University

Alpha Kappa Alpha Lineage

Initiated: Alpha Chi Chapter
North Carolina Central University-1968

South Valley Interest Group-1993

Theta Pi Omega, Epistoleus

Upsilon Delta Omega, 1994-Present
Charter Member

Offices Held: Tamiouchos, Ivy Leaf Reporter
Second Anti-Basileus, First Anti-Basileus,
Basileus

Distinctions: Graduated with honors from the
1st Ethel Hedgeman Lyle Leadership Academy
Class, North Atlantic Region, 2007

Chapter Officers

Basileus - Patricia McGhee
First Anti-Basileus - Gwendolyn Cobb
Second Anti-Basileus - Angela Lee
Grammateus - Erica Henderson
Epistoleus - Asha Ritchards
Tamiochous - Sheila Weeks Brown
Pecunious Grammateus - Sherry Ellis Knight
Ivy Leaf Reporter - Cheryl H. Butler
Hodegos/Philactor - LaSandra Watkins
Parliamentarian - Shabett Harper
Historian - Tina Browne Sills
Custodian - Brenda Dailey-Holmes
Chaplain - Veronica Wyatt

Chapter Members

Kamala Allen
Barbara R. Ashe
Terry L. Bell
Tasya Beck
Yvonne Tracie Boatwright
Claudia Brown
Natasha T. Brown
Dujuana Ambrose
Carla E. Wade-Elliott
Norma R. Evans
Jacqueline P. Flowers
Michelle Georgia
Jillian Hendricks

Lisa M. Jackson
Cassandra Poe-Johnson
Berdine Gordon-Littrean
Bethrotha A. Magee
Sharon Marshall
Gwendolyn A. Mills
Linda Robinson
Fe'Kere Thomas
LaGondia Barksdale-Tyler
Charisse Wheeler
Karen McGlashan-Williams
Diana Wright

Highlights of Soror Patricia McGhee
Fourth Upsilon Delta Omega Basileus

Upsilon Delta Omega Holds AKA Alarm Project

VOORHEES, NJ — During Fire Prevention Week, October 9-15, 2005, the chapter participated with the students from the Shirley B. Foster Elementary School in Chesilhurst, New Jersey. The theme this year was "Use Candles with Care" and each of the 5th and 6th grade participants was given a packet of information on fire prevention including the history of Fire Prevention Week, key points for kids, a home escape plan grid and a letter to parents in both English and Spanish. In addition, committee member, Soror Tracy Boatwright, made each participant a beautiful gift bag for the family containing an electric candle burner in addition to other gifts. The students read the list of key points for kids and discussed various points with Soror na Sills and Mary Ellen Tillmon. The students were told they would be given a quiz after the discussion and the two students with a perfect score

UPSILON DELTA OMEGA HOLDS ANNUAL YULETIDE BRUNCH

Voorhees, NJ — Upsilon Delta Omega held its Annual Yuletide Jazz Brunch on Sunday, December 7, 2008 at Aulettos Caterers in Almonesson, NJ. This afternoon affair was well attended by our sorors, their friends, and their families. There were numerous vendors, sorors and non-sorors highlighting Platform 1 — Entrepreneurship. Several guests walked away with door prizes. The purpose of this yearly event is to raise money for the scholarship fund.

Upsilon Delta Omega Holds AKA Children's Clothes Closet

CHERRY HILL, NJ — Upsilon Delta Omega Chapter in collaboration with the Woodland Avenue Presbyterian Church in Camden, New Jersey, the Rev. Floyd L. White, III, Pastor, sponsored its 4th Annual AKA Children's Clothes Closet on Saturday October 29, 2005. The chapter members donated and collected new and gently used clothing ranging in size from infant to young adult and distributed them to Camden residents. Many adults and children received much needed apparel which included, shirts, pants, skirts, shoes, sweaters several coats and other winter clothing. In addition to the distribution of the clothing, the event also hosted a "Fun Day" for children featuring clowns, a huge jungle gym and other entertainment. Voter registration information and forms were also available for residents.

Upsilon Delta Omega Hosts Its 13th Annual Yuletide Jazz Brunch

CHERRY HILL, NJ — On Sunday December 11, 2005, with an attendance of over 00 members, guests and supporters, the sorors of Upsilon Delta Omega chapter hosted its 13th Annual Yuletide Jazz Brunch at Auletto's Caterers in

Upsilon Delta Omega Kicks Off Its Ivy Reading AKAdemy

CHERRY HILL, NJ — Upsilon Delta Omega began its Ivy Reading AKAdemy program in November at the Elias Boudinot Elementary School in Burlington City, New Jersey. Each month the children are given two books, one that they are asked to read at home with their families and discuss at the next book club session; the second book is read aloud by a soror followed by an open-ended question and answer discussion session with the children. The January session honored Dr. Martin Luther King with a book entitled, *Dr. Martin Luther, Jr.* by David A. Adler being read and discussed. Through the discussion by a multicultural group of children, a better understanding and acceptance of each other was evidenced by the interaction of the children. In addition to the book reading, the children cut out a circle and colored it blue and brown representing the world, they then traced their hands and glued the hands to the world. The theme of the activity was "we hold our future". The children were served refreshments and given their books for the next session. The Ivy Reading Akademy book club is this chapter's avenue for providing educational community service to young students. Soror Sherry Ellis-Knight former principal of the elementary school coordinates the monthly sessions.

UPSILON DELTA OMEGA SPONSORS VOTER DRIVE

Voorhees, NJ — Members of Upsilon Delta Omega Chapter engaged its Voter Registration Campaign an all-day blitz. The chapter registered more an 60 English and Spanish speaking America uring the entire campaign. In addition to reg

Upsilon Delta Omega's MLK Day of Service

CHERRY HILL, NJ — The sorors of Upsilon Delta Omega Chapter captured the "Spirit of AKA" by hosting a Martin Luther King service project at the Anna M. Sample Family Shelter in Camden, New Jersey. The sorors and their children served lunch to the men, women and children residing at the shelter while everyone was engaging in cheerful and spirit-filled interaction. In addition, the sorors donated and distributed books, toys and toiletries to the residents who seemed very touched by the show of caring and sharing. This is an annual MLK community service project for the chapter. Chairperson and coordinator of this event was Soror LaSandra Watkins who with her committee and the support of the entire chapter planned and executed a very successful Martin Luther King Day of Service project.

Almonesson, New Jersey. The proceeds from this fund raising event provide scholarships for deserving local high school seniors, book awards for past scholarship recipients for the duration of their college experience and support for several of the chapter's community service programs. Also included in the festivities were several vendors with unique items for sale, including a large selection of African-American art, figurines, and statues. This festive event was highlighted with music by Love, Peace & Soul while guests enjoyed an exquisite buffet brunch. A plaque was given to Soror Betty Wilson, the Chapter's Golden Soror and to Mr. Jim Auletto, owner, in appreciation for his service to the chapter for thirteen years. Each visiting soror was given a pink rose, each guest was given a jazz brunch favor and many door prizes and giveaways were awarded. The event was a huge success under the leadership of Soror Patricia McGhee, Basileus, Sorors Erica Henderson and Cassandra Poe-Johnson, Jazz Brunch chair and co-chair, the Jazz Brunch Committee and the sisterly efforts of the entire chapter.

UPSILON DELTA OMEGA HONORS SCHOLARSHIP RECIPIENTS

Voorhees, NJ — Through its fundraising efforts, Upsilon Delta Omega Chapter continued its Enrich-Scholastic Program by awarding three $1,500 scholarships to three outstanding college-bound females. Recipients Efe Oghoghome, Joelle Tolifero and Christina Cameron will be attending the University of Pittsburg, West Chester University and Morgan State University respectively. In conjunction with our national target: promoting the success of the Black male, a $1,500 scholarship was also awarded to Michael Gregory who will be returning to the University of Hartford as a sophomore. All four recipi-

Patricia Y. McGhee

2005 - 2008

Patricia Yvonne McGhee served at basileus during a landmark time in African-American history. She began her first term as Basileus of Upsilon Delta Omega Chapter shortly before Condoleezza Rice was sworn in as U.S. Secretary of State - the first African-American woman to hold that office. Nearing the end of McGhee's second term as chapter Basileus, Barack Hussein Obama became the first African-American to be elected President of the United States. Patricia's vision as she took office was to stand for others who are most in need and to lead others to a stronger commitment of service. By implementing this vision, she led the chapter to stronger and more comprehensive involvement in the lives of homeless children and families.

Patricia's leadership style was best characterized as leading by example. She exhibited this style when she enrolled in the first nine-month long class of the Ethel Hedgeman Lyle Leadership Academy, to ensure that Upsilon Delta Omega Chapter was represented in the North Atlantic Region's inaugural class. Patricia motivated others to make great sacrifices through her willingness to take the lead in forfeiting her time, money and energy. These sacrifices were made in order to better meet the needs of the underserved in the chapter's local communities. Under her leadership, as a small chapter, Upsilon Delta Omega Chapter always worked harder and smarter. Coordinating and implementing VIP transportation from airports and shuttle service from four different hotels for the North Atlantic Regional Conference in Atlantic City, New Jersey, amounted to a herculean effort on the part of Upsilon Delta Omega Chapter. Members met the first buses at 6:00 AM every morning and saw the last buses back to the various hotels at 11:00 PM in the evening, and they did it with smiles on their faces knowing that their work was important to the overall success of the conference.

"A willingness to accept change, view tasks objectively and seek what is best for the overall good enhances productivity among those with common interests and goals."

In order to extend the chapter's impact on the community, Patricia realized that Upsilon Delta Omega Chapter needed to increase its involvement with other organizations whose practiced mission reflected those of Alpha Kappa Alpha Sorority Inc., and Upsilon Delta Omega Chapter. This vision was reflected in collaborations with Pi Mu Omega Chapter, Theta Pi Omega Chapter and other community-minded individuals, to organize and participate in voter registration drives throughout Burlington, Camden and Gloucester counties of New Jersey.

Serving as Basileus under both Supreme Basilei Linda Marie White and Barbara Anne McKinzie challenged Patricia to lead Upsilon Delta Omega Chapter in the implementation of new programs launched under those administrations. The chapter worked creatively to maintain valuable programs from the White administration, while implementing the new programs mandated by the McKinzie administration.

Patricia believed that a leader motivates, inspires and models. During her tenure as president of the chapter, Patricia exemplified those characteristics.

Patricia is married to Frederick McGhee and they have two sons, Khary and Zahir.

Gwendolyn T. Cobb

Born

April 17 – Tallahassee, Florida

Primary Vocation

Director, Education Bureau
NJ Real Estate Commission

Education

BA, Psychology, University of Southern California
CPM Designation, Rutgers University

Major Imprint in Office

- Initiated and oversaw the development of chapter's interactive website
- Encouraged chapter implementation of all national programs focusing on the areas of Financial Awareness, Entrepreneurship and Emerging Young Leaders
- Led chapter to award winning status for programs implemented in 2012
- Encouraged chapter participation on higher levels which led to a chapter record for members appointed to regional committees during her terms in office

Alpha Kappa Alpha Lineage

Initiated: Iota Beta Chapter, May 1977
University Southern California

Upsilon Delta Omega Chapter
2002-Present

Offices Held: Ivy Leaf Reporter, Second Anti-Basileus
First Anti-Basileus, Basileus

Regional Appointments:
Regional Protocol Committee
Chairman, Publicity Committee, NARC 2011
Transportation Committee, NARC 2005
NARC Workshop Facilitator

Chapter Officers

Basileus - Gwendolyn T. Cobb
First Anti-Basileus - Angela V. Lee
Second Anti-Basileus - Tina Browne Sills
Grammateus - Kamala Allen
Pecunious Grammateus - Fe'Kere Thomas
Anti-Pecunious Grammateus - Diana Wright
Tamiouchos - Shabett Harper
Anti-Tamiouchos - Sheila Weeks Brown
Epistoleus - Cheryl Butler
Hodegos - Charisse Wheeler
Philactor - Claudia Brown
Parliamentarian - Veronica Wyatt
Ivy Leaf Reporter - Dujuana Ambrose
Historian - Tracie Boatwright
Custodian/Keeper of Records - Brenda Dailey-Holmes
Chaplain - Charisse Wheeler

Chapter Members

Crystal Arthur	Lisa Jackson
Mia Bailey	Cassandra Poe-Johnson
Tasya Beck	Sherry Knight
Terry Bell	Berdine Gordan-Littrean
Diane Bruce	Bethrotha Magee
Maureen Carter	Rosalyn Mattingly
Leah DeCosta	Patricia M. McGhee
Norma R. Evans	Gwendolyn Mills
Jacqueline Flowers	Asha Richards
Michele Georgia	Linda Robinson
Krystin Gibson	Donna Walker
Erica Henderson	LaSandra Watkins
Jillian Hendricks	Karen McGlashan-Williams

Highlights of Soror Gwendolyn T. Cobb
Fifth Upsilon Delta Omega Basileus

UPSILON DELTA OMEGA HOSTS 17TH ANNUAL YULETIDE JAZZ BRUNCH

Voorhees, NJ — Members of Upsilon Delta Omega Chapter, family and friends gathered at Auletto Caterers, in Almonesson, NJ for the 17th Annual Yuletide Jazz Brunch. The Jazz Brunch is the premier event to raise money to support young people with scholarships. The chapter showcased seven entrepreneurs with a great selection of wares. The youngest vendor was Tyrus Ballard; he is a 16 year old entrepreneur, and finalist of

UPSILON DELTA OMEGA MARTIN LUTHER KING JR. DAY OF SERVICE

Cherry Hill, NJ — On Monday, January 18, 2010 fifteen ladies of Upsilon Delta Omega hosted the residents of Abigail House, an assisted living home, in Camden NJ in observance of Martin Luther King Jr Day. The residents of Abigail House and the sorors came together to sing songs reflective of Dr. King's work and the civil rights era. The residents shared stories about their memories of the late Dr. King, the impact of his work, and various reasons

UPSILON DELTA OMEGA SALUTES AFRICAN-AMERICAN MEN

Voorhees, NJ — Upsilon Delta Omega Chapter held its 9th Salute to African-American Men. During the afternoon affair 13 honorees, eight mentors and five young men, which exemplify the importance of service to the community and/or education were recognized. Male Mentors: David Burgess, Virgil Carmen, Darryl T. Curtis, Derek Davis, Chad D. King,

THETA PI OMEGA HOLDS HEALTH & ECONOMIC SMART FAIR

orestown NJ — Theta Pi Omega Chapter collabo ed with local chapters Pi Mu Omega, Willingbor ., and Upsilon Delta Omega, Voorhees, NJ, plement an Extraordinary Service Project und auspice of Platform II, The Economic Keys

UPSILON DELTA OMEGA HOLDS FAMILY FUN DAY

Voorhees, NJ — In an effort to bring some joy and fun to families who have fallen on hard times, members of Upsilon Delta Omega Chapter hosted their annual Family Fun Day at the Anna M. Sample Family Shelter. The Family Fun Day event was coordinated by Sorors Asha Richards and Cassandra Poe-Johnson under the leadership of the

UPSILON DELTA OMEGA PRESENTS SOCIAL JUSTICE AND HUMAN RIGHTS WORKSHOP

Voorhees, NJ — Members of Upsilon Delta Omega Chapter under the leadership of Basileus Gwendolyn Cobb serving the woman of the Good Counsel Home presented a workshop entitled, Domestic Violence—How to Grow After the Drama. Sorors and guests served lunch to six residents of the home, got acquainted with the young women and presented an informative presentation entitled Domestic Violence- How to Grow After the Drama, providing a wealth of information to the residents. After the presentation, questions were answered and the residents shared the experiences. Next, the women were given a packet of information which included agencies and locations where victims of domestic violence could get help; some of the residents requested one-on-one meetings with the sorors to obtain information about their particular interests and issues. Finally, each resident was presented with a box of chocolates in honor of Valentine's Day and Heart Health Month.

AN EXCLUSIVE INTERNATIONAL WOMEN'S DAY EVENT WITH UPSILON DELTA OMEGA

Voorhees, NJ — On the evening of Thursday, March 5th, 2009 five sorors from Upsilon Delta Omega had 10 young women represented from Winslow Township H.S., along with their school counselor join them in attending the acclaimed documentary, "A Powerful Noise Live" and a live town hall discussion at the Ritz Theatre in Voorhees, NJ. This movie followed three women — Hanh in Vietnam who's story reveals "that when women become

UPSILON DELTA OMEGA AND S.T.A.R.S FOUNDATION PRESENT 18TH ANNUAL JAZZ BRUNCH

ees, NJ — S. T. A. R. S. (Sisters That Are Rendering Service) in conjunction with the Upsilon Delta Omega Chapter hel l scholarship fundraiser — the 18th Annual Yuletide h. The Yuletide Jazz Brunch chairwoman was Soror Lisa Ja

The Timeless Service of Upsilon Delta Omega Chapter

Gwendolyn T. Cobb

2009 - 2012

Upsilon Delta Omega's fifth chapter President always had a calm and positive personality. Her perspective on life was that the "glass is always half full" regardless of what a situation may look like. Optimism was the foundation of her leadership style.

Gwendolyn made a commitment to community service and leadership at a young age as she observed her grandmother volunteer her time and help others in need. This developed in Gwendolyn the belief that part of her own purpose on this earth was to commit to a lifetime of community service and in 1977 she chose to do that through Alpha Kappa Alpha Sorority, Inc.

"We all have been placed on this earth, at this time for a reason. I believe that one is not truly satisfied in life until they know in their heart that they are fulfilling at least some of what God's will is for them as they inhabit this earth."

One of Gwendolyn's goals was to encourage members to get involved in Alpha Kappa Alpha beyond the chapter level and because of that, the chapter had its largest number of members appointed to serve on a variety of regional committees as she also was appointed to the Regional Protocol Committee during that time.

The implementation of all the national programs could be a daunting task, especially with the challenges faced by a small chapter. However, with encouragement and a "hands on" approach, Gwendolyn didn't mind getting in the trenches even if it meant rolling up her sleeves and getting a little green on her pink. This mindset led to the successful execution of programs for 2012 that led the chapter to win the "Overall Outstanding Chapter of the Year" award at the 2013 North Atlantic Regional Conference.

Gwendolyn added her signature to the core chapter programs by starting an "Adopt a Military Family" committee. This program also aligned with that of First Lady Michelle Obama, to support current and retired military personnel. The chapter also adopted the Good Counsel Home which provides shelter and other services for unwed expectant mothers and their children.

A firm believer in the benefits of technology, Gwendolyn was the catalyst in developing the chapter's first interactive website. This vehicle highlighted the community service projects and the impact that the chapter had on the people that were served. Focusing on "going green" this tool offered areas that members utilized for planning and conducting the business of Alpha Kappa Alpha Sorority, Inc.

Gwendolyn also chaired the Publicity Committee for the 2011 North Atlantic Regional Conference. She directed the committee in the successful development of various means of communication via social media, radio, print and photography.

Gwendolyn's supportive family includes her husband, Garry, and their three adult children, Allie, Garry II and Allyse. They also have three grandchildren, Azlan, Rayna and Vivien.

Angela V. Lee

Born

April 7 - Durham, NC

Primary Vocation

Training Coordinator
New Jersey Child Support Institute,
Rutgers University

Education

BBA, Accounting, Howard University
MA, Educational Psychology,
Rowan University

Major Imprint in Office

- Led the chapter in growth from 25 members to 36 members
- Guided the chapter in the implementation of current National Initiatives
- As Program Chair, she was the guiding force to Upsilon Delta Omega being recognized with the regional award for "Overall Outstanding Chapter of the Year"
- Received an award for Outstanding Soror in 2008
- Encouraged minority entrepreneurial growth by creating the AKArd Exchange networking event.
- Expanding Upsilon Delta Omega Chapter's collaboration with neighboring chapters on various National Program Initiatives
- Committed chapter to efforts to "Go Green" and encouraged use of electronic tools.

Alpha Kappa Alpha Lineage

Initiated: Xi Omega Chapter, April 1992
Washington, D.C.

Upsilon Delta Omega Chapter
2002–Present

Offices Held: Epistoleus, Parliamentarian, Second Anti-Basileus, First Anti-Basileus, Basileus

Regional Appointments:

Regional Corporate Sponsorship Committee

Chairman, Graphics, Signs, Banners, and Printing Committee, NARC 2011

Transportation Committee, NARC 2005

NARC Workshop Facilitator

Chapter Officers

Basileus - Angela V. Lee
1st Anti Basileus - Tina Browne Sills
2nd Anti Basileus - Shabett Harper
Grammateus - Kamala Allen
Anti-Grammateus - Cheryl Butler
Pecunious Grammateus - Dujuana Ambrose
Tamiouchos - Leah DeCosta
Anti-Tamiouchos - Sheila Weeks Brown
Epistoleus - Cheryl Butler
Hodegos - Charisse Wheeler
Philactor - Veronica Wyatt
Parliamentarian - Roslyn Myers
Ivy Leaf Reporter - Kamala Allen
Chaplin - Charisse Wheeler
Historian - Donna Walker
Custodian Keeper of Records - Yvonne Tracie Boatwright

Chapter Members

Tonya Adams	Kathy Glass
Nikita Brantley	Carla Harris
Laila Brooks-Mitchell	Kameelah Majied
Claudia Brown	Patricia McGhee
Diane Bruce	Natasha McSeed
Brenda Dailey-Holmes	Tania Morgan
Norma Evans	Cassandra Poe-Johnson
Venessa Fanning	Fe'Kere Thomas
Deneise Fuller	LaSandra Watkins
Jovita Gale	Karen Williams

Highlights of Soror Angela V. Lee
Sixth Upsilon Delta Omega Basileus

UPSILON DELTA OMEGA SERVES COMMUNITY

Cherry Hill, NJ — For Upsilon Delta Omega Chapter, the first half of 2013 was full of community service projects and execution of the Supreme Basileus' program priorities. In January, sorors participated in the MLK Day of Service at the Willingboro Public Library, donating food items for local pantries and supplies for local animal shelters. For February's Pink Goes Red, the chapter conducted a heart health awareness workshop for residents of the Good Counsel Home in Riverside, NJ, which provides a safe, nurturing residence for young, homeless, pregnant women who stay at the home through their child's first birthday. In April, the chapter sponsored a two-hour session. In May, the chapter sponsored a team in the Delran NJ Relay for Life, overnight community fundraising/walk to combat cancer. Sorors raised $1,590. Finally, in June, the annual Scholarship Luncheon at the Moorestown Community House in Moorestown, NJ, was held to award $6,000 in college scholarships to young women who exhibited scholastic excellence in their high school careers. Each member of Upsilon Delta Omega Chapter provided the scholarship recipients with words of encouragement and insight from her own college experience. The S.T.A.R.S. Foundation, the charitable arm of Upsilon Delta Omega Chapter, provides these scholarships through its annual fundraising effort, the Yuletide Jazz Brunch, now in its 21st year.

PINK GOES RED AT THE GOOD COUNSEL HOME

Members of Upsilon Delta Omega Chapter converged at the Good Counsel Home in Riverside, NJ, on Monday, February 4, 2013 to deliver a Healthy Heart Awareness workshop in keeping with the goals of Pink Goes Red. The Good Counsel Home's primary mission is to provide shelter and assistance to homeless pregnant women by providing a loving family environment in a safe and secure environment. They teach various life skills that prepare them to become self sufficient. Chapter members held a viewing of the American Heart Association's 2013 Women Go Red "Our Story: For Women, By Women" presentation,

Young mothers at the Good Counsel Home listen attentively to a heart health presentation from members of Upsilon Delta Omega Chapter. Their faces were intentionally not photographed to protect their identities.

and served the young mothers an assortment of red heart healthy snacks. They, along with the staff of this residential program, were also instructed on how to read food labels properly, told the importance of knowing their blood pressure and cholesterol levels, and given tips on how to recognize heart attack and stroke symptoms in women. This was a very interactive session with a lively discussion and a question and answer period. Each participant received a packet of handouts and heart healthy

Panel sounds fresh warning over human trafficking

Douglas was joined on the panel by state Assistant Attorney General Tracy Thompson; Rev. Leslie R. Harrison, of the Bethel African Methodist Episcopal Church in Moorestown; and Dr. Mario Tommasi of South Jersey-based Community Treatment Solutions. Texas Attorney General Greg Abbott -- whose state hosted the big game in 2011 -- told USA Today the Super Bowl is "commonly known as the single- largest human trafficking incident in the United States

SORORS AND EMERGING YOUNG LEADERS PARTICIPATE IN 3-PRONGED MLK DAY OF SERVICE

In recognition of the Day of Service, Upsilon Delta Omega Chapter participated in a local event at the Burlington County Library in Burlington, NJ. On this day, three community service events were conducted simultaneously. Chapter members and other individuals from the community donated food items to the local homeless shelter, as well as food and pet care items for the local animal shelter. Upsilon Delta Omega chose to make this event one of the monthly activities for its Emerging Young Leaders, several of whom brought donations for both the homeless shelter and for the sheltered animals. Chapter members and the EYL participants also created many hand-made personal greeting cards for residents of area convalescent homes designed to bring them inspirational

MARTIN LUTHER KING DAY OF SERVICE

Pi Epsilon Chapter came together with the ladies of Rho Theta Omega Chapter at Girard College in Philadelphia, PA on January 21, 2013 to celebrate the Martin Luther King Day of Service. Our goal was to support the Social Justice Initiative. We wrote letters to military servicemen and women, to their families, and donated school supplies to children who go to military schools. Donations of books were also made for the libraries on military bases. We came together to show the support we have for our troops as well as our community. The ladies of Alpha Kappa Alpha Sorority, Inc. took the initiative to show that we are about global leadership through timeless service.

2013 Yuletide Jazz Brunch

On December 8, 2013, Upsilon Delta Omega Chapter held its 2013 Yuletide Jazz Brunch at Auletto Caterers in Deptford, NJ. The Brunch is the chapter's annual fundraising gala to support its college scholarships, which are awarded each spring to young women who exhibit scholastic excellence in their high school careers and have been accepted to 4-year colleges and universities for the coming fall semester. This year's event was planned to host 300 guests and included a lavish brunch buffet. While an unexpected winter storm hit on the morning of the event, the chapter pushed through and the event went on. The program featured great music by Philadelphia's Blind Date Band, a "Pink Carpet" Photo Experience, and vendors offering a range of exquisite items including jewelry, fine art, paraphernalia, and clothing and other personal items. Additionally, in the last quarter of the year, the chapter co-sponsored a community education workshop on Human Trafficking with three other chapters with over 100 attendees and coverage in the local media. UDO also launched the new school year for its Emerging Young Leaders with an interactive ice cream social. The girls spent time learning about the program and getting to know the chapter and each other. The chapter also welcomed six new sorors into the Alpha Kappa Alpha Sorority in October. All and all, it was a very productive quarter for Upsilon Delta Omega.

UPSILON DELTA OMEGA PRESENTS SOCIAL JUSTICE AND HUMAN RIGHTS WORKSHOP

Voorhees, NJ — Members of Upsilon Delta Omega Chapter under the leadership of Basileus Gwendolyn Cobb served the women of the Good Counsel Home presented a workshop entitled, Domestic Violence—How to Grow After the Drama. Sorors and guests served lunch to six residents at the home, got acquainted with the young women and presented an informative presentation entitled Domestic Violence: How to Grow After the Drama, providing a wealth of information to the residents. After the presentation, questions were answered and the residents shared their experiences. Next, the women were given a packet of information which included agencies and locations where victims of domestic violence could get help; some of the residents requested one-on-one meetings with the sorors to obtain information about their particular interests and issues. Finally, each resident was presented with a box of chocolates in honor of Valentine's Day and Heart Health Month.

The Timeless Service of Upsilon Delta Omega Chapter

Angela V. Lee

2013 - Present

Angela Lee, the sixth Basileus of Upsilon Delta Omega Chapter (UDO), joined the chapter in 2002. With less than a year in the chapter, she was asked to serve as Epistoleus, in addition to chairing various chapter committees. From that point forward, she was nominated to officer positions leading up to the role of Basileus. She began her term as president in January 2013 with a total of 25 members in the chapter. After several transfers, reactivations and a Membership Intake Process, she grew the chapter to 36 members before the end of the year.

During her first year, she led the chapter to very successfully serve the community and address all six of the program initiatives laid out by the Supreme Basileus Carolyn House Stewart. During her term the chapter won the regional award "Overall Outstanding Chapter of the Year," confirming what she always felt about UDO and its members. This was an amazing feat for a small chapter such as UDO to be recognized with this award given all of the other chapters in the region that competed for the award, including chapters much larger than UDO. This award was for the 2012 year, when Angela was the Program Chair and responsible for managing the program initiative committees and activities in the chapter. The award was a great testament to her leadership success as program chair.

During Angela's term, she focused on improving the ability to manage chapter operations by updating the chapter bylaws to include more technology-centered rules appropriate for the time and environment. Her goal was to ensure that the chapter was technologically prepared for the future.

"If you always do what you always did, you will always have what you always had."

Angela served as Chair of the Graphics, Banners, Posters, and Printing committee for the 2011 North Atlantic Regional Conference, overseeing the vendor selection and all of the printer related activities including creating all of the banners and posters for the entire conference. She also served on the North Atlantic Regional Corporate Sponsorship committee from 2011 and 2012. She also worked on several award submissions for the chapter, including a display that won 3rd place at NARC 2006. From the beginning, Angela's commitment to Alpha Kappa Alpha Sorority, Inc., and in turn, Upsilon Delta Omega has been, without hesitation, a major priority for her. It is no wonder that in 2008, she was honored with the chapter's award for "Outstanding Soror" in light of her never-ending energy and commitment to UDO.

One of Angela's goal has always been working smarter to serve the community, address the international program initiatives and promote sisterhood, while not exhausting chapter resources. She appreciates the commitment and devotion of her chapter members, but also understands the realities and demands of their personal lives and how that may impact their ability to be constantly available for projects. In response, she is constantly trying to figure out new ways to get things done. One of her favorite Bible quotes is from Psalms 46:10, "Be still, and know that I am God." At the time of this writing, Angela is engaged to be married to Mr. Vernell Watson.

Upsilon Delta Omega

Chapter Member

Profiles

2013

Tonya Adams

AKA Initiation: *2013, Upsilon Delta Omega Chapter*
Degree(s): *BA, Communication Management, University Dayton;*
MS, Information Systems, DePaul University
Current Profession: *Director, Commercial Network Operations*

"Alpha Kappa Alpha, Inc., is a sisterhood and bond that cannot and will never be broken, as we stand strong like the Ivy, united as one, persevering through any and all obstacles and most importantly giving to others unselfishly."

Quote: "I can do all things through Christ which strengtheneth me." Philippians 4:13 "No weapon that is formed against thee shall prosper." Isaiah 54:17

Kamala Allen

AKA Initiation: *1990, Alpha Gamma Chapter*
Degree(s): *BA, Psychology, University of California, Los Angeles;*
MHS, Maternal and Child Health, Johns Hopkins Bloomberg School
of Public Health
Current Profession: *Vice President, Program Operations*
Offices Held: *Second Anti-Basileus, Grammateus, Ivy Leaf Reporter*
UDO Membership: *1997*

"Membership in Alpha Kappa Alpha Sorority, Inc., means a lifelong, meaningful relationship with like-minded women who are committed to improving the lives of girls, women and communities. There is no other like our sisterhood."

Quote: "You are braver than you believe, stronger than you seem, and smarter than you think." – Christopher Robin

Dujuana Ambrose-Dessau

AKA Initiation: 1997, Iota Tau Omega Chapter
Degree(s): BS, Elementary/Early Childhood Education, Millersville University; MA, Educational Administration, Cheyney University
Current Profession: Elementary Principal
Offices Held: Ivy Leaf Reporter; Pecunious Grammateus
UDO Membership: 2007

"My work with Alpha Kappa Alpha Sorority, Inc., gives me the opportunity to work with women that love to give back to the community. I made the best choice!"

Quote: "I need to have a good laugh every day."

Yvonne Tracie Boatwright

AKA Initiation: 1996, Upsilon Delta Omega Chapter
Degree(s): BA, Psychology, Rutgers University
Current Profession: Homemaker
Offices Held: Hodegos, Historian, Custodian

"Alpha Kappa Alpha to me means sisterhood and upholding the mission of our founders."

Quote: "Success is loving life and daring to live it." Maya Angelou

Nikita D. Brantley

AKA Initiation: 2013, Upsilon Delta Omega Chapter
Degree(s): BA, Sociology, Montclair State University; MA, Social Work, Rutgers University
Current Profession: Casework Supervisor for the State of New Jersey

"Alpha Kappa Alpha Sorority Inc., to me means selflessly providing service to the community. AKA means there is hope for those who are in need, there is love for those who dare to receive it, and a sisterhood available to stand strong with me through it all."

Quote: "God doesn't test the strength of his soldiers by giving them easy tasks." ~unknown~

Laila S. Brooks-Mitchell

AKA Initiation: 2013, Upsilon Delta Omega Chapter
Degree(s): BA, Psychology, Rutgers University; - MA, Psychology, University of Phoenix
Current Profession: Adoption Caseworker for the State of New Jersey

"Alpha Kappa Alpha means everything to me. It is a faithful and loving sisterhood in which we use our love for each other to unite, cultivate and serve the community in which we live."

Quote: "But they that wait upon the Lord shall renew their strength; they shall mount up with wings as eagles; they shall run, and not be weary; and they shall walk and not faint." Isaiah 40:31

Claudia Brown

AKA Initiation: *1995, Gamma Zeta Chapter*
Degree(s): *BA, Social Work, Rutgers University*
Current Profession: *Business Analyst*

"It seems so cliché, but AKA truly means a lifetime of love, sisterhood, friendship and service to all mankind. It is one of the best decisions I have ever made in my life."

Quote: "There comes a time when you walk away from drama and all of the people who create it. Surround yourself with people who make you laugh, forget the bad and focus on the good. Love the people who treat you right. Pray for the ones who don't. Life is too short to be anything but happy. Falling down is part of life, but getting up is living."

Sheila Weeks Brown

AKA Initiation: *2003, Upsilon Delta Omega Chapter*
Degree(s): *BS, Business Administration, Howard University*
Current Profession: *Vice President, Finance*
Offices Held: *Tamiouchos, Anti-Tamiouchos, Epistoleus*

"Alpha Kappa Alpha means to me a sister that has your back during the good and the not so good times!"

Quote: "And do not be conformed to this world, but be transformed by the renewing of your mind that you may prove what is that good and acceptable and perfect will of God." Romans 12:2

Diane Bruce

AKA Initiation: *1971, Delta Lambda Chapter*
Degree(s): *BA, Sociology, MA, Social Work, Delaware State University*
Current Profession: *School Social Worker*
Offices Held: *Historian*
UDO Membership: *1994*
Distinctions: *Silver Star, Charter Member - Upsilon Delta Omega Chapter*

"Alpha Kappa Alpha Sorority, Inc., means for me sisterhood, love of God and service to mankind."

Quote: "Trust in the Lord with all thine heart; and lean not unto thine own understanding." Proverbs 3:5

Cheryl H. Butler

AKA Initiation: *1979, Delta Alpha Chapter*
Degree(s): *BS, Business Education, Fayetteville State University; MA, Education, Gratz College*
Current Profession: *Retired High School Business Education Teacher/Department Chair*
Offices Held: *Grammateus, Ivy Leaf Reporter, Epistoleus*
UDO Membership: *1994*
Distinctions: *Silver Star, Charter Member - Upsilon Delta Omega Chapter*

"Alpha Kappa Alpha Sorority, Inc., is the epitome of sisterly relations and service to all mankind."

Quote: "I do not at all understand the mystery and miracle of grace, only that it meets us where we are but does not leave us where it found us."

Brenda A. Dailey-Holmes

AKA Initiation: *1985, Beta Chapter*
Degree(s): *BS, Chemical Engineering, Illinois Institute of Technology - Chicago; MS, Engineering Management, Drexel University*
Current Profession: *Engineer*
Offices Held: *Tamiouchos, Custodian*
UDO Membership: *1997*
Distinctions: *Silver Star, Life Member*

"Alpha Kappa Alpha Sorority, Inc., means to me a lifelong commitment of providing service to mankind, by continuing the examples of our Founders while implementing strategies of today."

Quote: "Be anxious for nothing, but in everything by prayer and supplication, with thanksgiving, let your requests be made known to God." Philippians 4:6

Leah DeCosta

AKA Initiation: *2007, Iota Psi Chapter*
Degree(s): *BS, Economics, Rutgers University*
Current Profession: *Contracting Officer for the U.S. General Services Administration*
Offices Held: *Tamiouchos*
UDO Membership: *2008*

"Alpha Kappa Alpha Sorority, Inc., is a group of empowered women working together to achieve the same mission. It represents sisterhood, love, support, work ethic, forgiveness, empathy, and character. The sorority provides an outlet to serve and uplift the community and that is our primary focus."

Quote: "Women who understand how powerful they are do not give into envy over meaningless things; instead they fight to maintain the beautiful bond of the sisterhood." – Bindi

Venessa Fanning

AKA Initiation: *2013, Upsilon Delta Omega Chapter*
Degree(s): *AS, Nursing, Gwynedd Mercy University; BS, Community Health Education, East Stroudsburg University*
Current Profession: *Registered Nurse*

"Alpha Kappa Alpha Sorority, Inc., means to me a sisterhood united, identifying specific needs within the community while bringing about positive change in the community."

Quote: "Be still, and know that I am God; I will be exalted among the nations, I will be exalted in the earth." Psalms 46:10

Deneise Fuller

AKA Initiation: *2012, Sigma Zeta Omega Chapter*
Degree(s): *BS, Management, Rutgers University School of Business*
Current Profession: *Administrative Specialist*
UDO Membership: *2013*

"I believe Alpha Kappa Alpha Sorority, Inc., signifies a sisterhood amongst a group of outstanding women committed to the work of uplifting our communities and one another. AKA exemplifies purpose, faith and sisterhood."

Quote: "We can't solve problems by using the same kind of thinking we used when we created them."
– Albert Einstein

Jovita Gale

AKA Initiation: *2003, Lambda Upsilon Omega Chapter*
Degree(s): *BA, Biology/Chemistry, Johnson C. Smith University*
Current Position: *Clinical Research Professional*
UDO Membership: *2013*

"Membership in Alpha Kappa Alpha Sorority Inc., means a sisterhood empowered to serve!"

Quote: "As we are liberated from our own fear, our presence automatically liberates others." – Marianne Williamson

Kathy Glass

AKA Initiation: *2013, Upsilon Delta Omega Chapter*
Degree(s): *BS, Business Administration, Bowie State University*
Current Profession: *IT Compliance and Oversight Specialist*

"Alpha Kappa Alpha Sorority is to me a sisterhood of love and unity while working together to make a difference for mankind."

Quote: "I can do all things through Christ which strengtheneth me." Philippians 4:13

Shabett Harper

AKA Initiation: 1993, Epsilon Nu Chapter
Degree(s): BS, Accounting, Lincoln University; MHA, Healthcare Administration, Seton Hall University
Current Profession: Government Contract Auditor
Offices Held: Second Anti-Basileus, Tamiouchos, Parliamentarian, Philactor, Hodegos, and Grammateus
UDO Membership: 1997

"Alpha Kappa Alpha Sorority, Inc., means working together to build sisterhood as we provide services to build our communities."

Quote: "Do unto others as you would have them do unto you." Luke 6:31

Carla Harris

AKA Initiation: 1983, Iota Beta Chapter
Degree(s): BS, Architecture, Temple University; BS, Allied Health, Charles Drew University; Masters in Medical Science, Alderson Broaddus University
Current Profession: Physician Assistant
UDO Membership: 2013
Distinctions: Silver Star

"Being a member of Alpha Kappa Alpha was something I strived for as an elementary school student. I observed the Sisterhood while visiting my sister's college at that age. I saw the Sisterhood, the friendships, the community service, the sharing and caring, all of which I wanted to be a part of. I have also been supported through my many endeavors and being a part of the AKA Sisterhood gives me a chance to give back and be someone's Sister/Soror, mentor and friend."

Quote: "You may encounter many defeats, but you must not be defeated." - Maya Angelou

Sherry Ellis-Knight

AKA Initiation: 1996, Upsilon Delta Omega Chapter
Degree(s): BA, Elementary Education, Mississippi State University; MA, Educational Leadership, Cheyney University
Current Position: Elementary School Principal
Offices Held: Grammateus, Anti-Grammateus, Pecunious Grammateus, Tamiouchos

"Alpha Kappa Alpha, Inc., is a bond of sisterhood that is truly like no other. This sisterhood is one of dedication, loyalty and support."

Quote: "In order to succeed, your desire for success must be greater than your fear of failure."

Sheila Linton

AKA Initiation: 1970, Delta Gamma Chapter
Degree(s): BA, Science Education, MS, Library and Information Science, Pennsylvania State University
Current Profession: Retired Educator
Offices Held: Member-At-Large
UDO Membership: 2013
Distinctions: Silver Star

"Alpha Kappa Alpha has allowed me to have life-long friends, network with sorors in various states and provide worthwhile community service to those in need."

Quote: "To teach is to touch a life forever." Anonymous

Bethrotha Magee

AKA Initiation: 2007, Upsilon Delta Omega Chapter
Degree(s): BA, Elementary Education; MA, Elementary Education and Administration, Cheyney University

Alpha Kappa Alpha Sorority Inc., affords me the opportunity to become more involved with the community and serve mankind. The sisterhood is most uplifting. I am proud to be a member of Alpha Kappa Alpha Sorority, Incorporated."

Kameelah S. Majied

AKA Initiation: 2013, Upsilon Delta Omega Chapter
Degree(s): Bachelor of Engineering in Mechanical Engineering, MS, Project Management, Stevens Institute of Technology
Current Profession: Business and Technology Strategist

"Alpha Kappa Alpha Sorority, Inc., means uniquely bonded in sisterhood and working with outstanding women, to change society; one citizen at a time. In this bond, we collectively guide people in truly reaching and realizing their capabilities, and improving their lives."

Quote: "Success is when you realize the very things that you truly are capable of doing."

Rosalyn Myers

AKA Initiation: *1986, Epsilon Beta Omega Chapter*
Degree(s): *BA, Political Science, University of South Carolina;*
Juris Doctor, Tulane University Law School
Current Profession: *Attorney*
Offices Held: *Parliamentarian*
UDO Membership: *2010*

"AKA means sisterliness, community service, teamwork and fun."

Quote: "Be the change you want to see in the world." – Gandhi

Cassandra Poe-Johnson

AKA Initiation: *1986, Epsilon Nu Chapter*
Degree(s): *BA, Human Services and Sociology; MS,*
Administration, Lincoln University
Current Profession: *New Jersey Agency Administrator*
Offices Held: *Anti-Grammateus*
UDO Membership: *1995*
Distinctions: *Silver Star, Life Member*

"Alpha Kappa Alpha Sorority, Inc., has allowed me the opportunity to be sisters with such a beautiful array of intelligent ladies who have similar interests to my own. I thank God so much for blessing me with this sisterhood. I am ever so thankful and humble that I have lived more than half of my life as a member of Alpha Kappa Alpha Sorority, Inc."

Quote: "Give the world the best you have and it may never be enough; Give the world the best you've got anyway. You see, in the final analysis, it is between you and your God; it was never between you and them anyway." – Mother Teresa

Tina Browne Sills

AKA Initiation: 1970, Alpha Chapter
Degree(s): BS, Psychology, Howard University; MA, Student Personnel Services, Glassboro State College
Current Profession: School Counselor
Offices Held: Historian, Anti-Pecunious Grammateus, Epistoleus, Foundation Board Member, Second Anti-Basileus, and First Anti-Basileus
UDO Membership: 1995
Distinctions: Silver Star, Life Member, Graduate of the 2010 Ethel Hedgeman Lyle Leadership Academy, Member of the 2013 Anne Mitchem Davis Officers Institute, 2011 Member of the North Atlantic Region Nominating Committee, 2013 Member of the North Atlantic Region Program Committee, 2011 North Atlantic Regional Conference Vice-Chair of Graphics, Banners, Signs & Printing Committee

"Alpha Kappa Alpha Sorority, Inc., is a lifelong sisterhood of women with a shared love of the sorority and a commitment to serve all mankind."

Quote: "I can do things you cannot, you can do things I cannot; together we can do great things." – Mother Teresa

Fe'Kere Thomas

AKA Initiation: 2007, Upsilon Delta Omega Chapter
Degree(s): BA, Journalism and Mass Media; MA Communication and Information Studies, Rutgers University
Current Profession: Public Relations/Corporate Communication
Offices Held: Pecunious Grammateus

"Alpha Kappa Alpha Sorority Inc., means strength and allegiance through sisterhood. As an AKA, there is always someone who will support you, stand by you and with you, and help guide you through every aspect of life like work, family, and community."

Quote: "Because there's one thing stronger than magic: sisterhood." – Robin Benway

Donna Walker

AKA Initiation: 1997, Iota Tau Omega Chapter
Degree(s): BA, Social Work, Millersville; MA Education,
University of Pennsylvania
Current Profession: Child Study Team School Social Worker
Offices Held: Historian
UDO Membership: 2010

"Alpha Kappa Alpha Sorority, Inc, is an unbreakable bond sisterhood of women around the world that share a commitment to serve mankind. AKA is something I can count on for the rest of my life."

Quote: "Excuses are tools for the incompetent which build monuments of nothingness. Those that use them seldom amount to anything." – Stephen Grayhm

Charisse Y. Wheeler

AKA Initiation: 1985, Epsilon Nu Chapter
Degee(s): BA, Clinical Psychology, Lincoln University;
MSW, Social Work, Rutgers University
Current Profession: Social Work Administrator
Offices Held: Chaplain, Hodegos
UDO Membership: 2006
Distinctions: Silver Star

"Alpha Kappa Alpha Sorority Inc., means to me an opportunity to become an agent of change within our community, an inward passion to serve and an outward beacon of light to those dark places of hopelessness. AKA means sisterhood and friendships among beautiful sorors. Finally it means to empower, embrace and strengthen others."

Quote: "I can do all things through Christ who gives me strength." Philippians 4:13.

LaSandra Watkins

AKA Initiation: 2003, Upsilon Delta Omega Chapter
Degree(s): BS, Biology, Alcorn State University; MA, Educational Leadership and EdD, Educational Leadership, Rowan University
Current Profession: Retired Educator
Offices Held: Ivy Leaf Reporter, Tamiouchos
Distinctions: Graduate of the Ethel Hedgeman Lyle Leadership Academy

"Alpha Kappa Alpha represents an organization whose mission is to perpetuate and lift up the true meaning of sisterhood."

Quote: "Every word of God is pure; he is a shield unto them that put their trust in him. Add thou not unto his words, lest he reprove thee, and thou be found a liar." Proverbs 30:5-6

Karen McGlashan Williams

AKA Initiation: 1984, Delta Gamma Chapter
Degree(s): BS, Administration of Justice, Pennsylvania State University; JD, Law, Temple University Beasley School of Law
Current Profession: Legal
Offices Held: Parliamentarian
UDO Membership: 1994
Distinctions: Silver Star, Charter Member of Upsilon Delta Omega Chapter

"Alpha Kappa Alpha Sorority means sisterhood to me."

Quote: "To whom much is given much is expected in return." "We are but temporary caregivers of this earth. Therefore we should each leave a mark that improves the species, places and persons we leave behind."

Veronica Wyatt

AKA: Initiation: 1980, Theta Tau Omega Chapter
Degree(s): BS, Business Education, University of Bridgeport
Current Profession: Senior Procurement Manager
Offices Held: Chaplain, Parliamentarian, Philactor
UDO Membership: 2006
Distinctions: Silver Star

"Alpha Kappa Alpha Sorority is a sisterhood that is unconditional and a relationship with extraordinary women that is like no other. Words cannot describe the greatness and our commitment and service to mankind."

Quote: "I smile with my eyes, laugh with my heart and love with my soul."

Yuletide Jazz Brunch

The chapter's annual Yuletide Jazz Brunch - held since its inception in 1992 at Auletto Caterers in Deptford, NJ - is in its 22nd year at the time of this printing. The Brunch is the chapter's annual fundraising gala to support its college scholarship program, which awards several scholarships to exceptional young women and men who are graduating high school with distinction. The awards allow the recipients to offset the cost of books or other education-related expenses. Funds raised at this event also sponsor several of the community service projects that the chapter hosts throughout the year. Annually, the Jazz Brunch hosts between 250-300 guests and features a lavish brunch buffet, great live music by a regional band, and vendors offering a range of exquisite items including jewelry, fine art, paraphernalia, clothing and other accessories. Most recently, the chapter added a "Pink Carpet" Photo Experience, so guests could memorialize the event with a custom photo on the Upsilon Delta Omega Pink Carpet.

UPSILON DELTA OMEGA CHAPTER
YULETIDE JAZZ BRUNCH
(*Through the Years*)

Salute To African-American Men

The Salute is an Upsilon Delta Omega (UDO) chapter program initiated in 1996 to honor African-American men who devote their time and energy, giving back to our youth and communities. UDO created the Salute to empower the black family by celebrating the role of African-American men as integral contributors to our families and communities. The chapter believed it was important to put a different message out to the community-at-large about the great work being done by African-American men to foster the well-being of their communities, in contrast to the stereotypical message portrayed by the mainstream media. To-date, UDO has hosted 10 Salutes, honoring both accomplished adult males and in several years, also recognizing "Rising Stars" - young men who have demonstrated great promise. Categories of accomplishment have included - Education, Religion, Law and Justice, Sports, and others. All profits generated from the Salute are used to fund various UDO community service projects which continue its legacy of Service to All Mankind.

UPSILON DELTA OMEGA CHAPTER SALUTES
AFRICAN AMERICAN MEN

Salute 1996

Salute 1998

Cochran speaks to gala crowd

Men Of

> *S*tature

> *A*uthority

> *L*atitude

> *U*nderstanding

> *T*alent

> *E*ndless
  Accomplishments

Salute 2000

Salute 2002

Salute 2006

Salute 2009

Salute 2012

Top of the Game • International Women's Day • Buckle Up • Shoebox Project • Bowling Party • Domestic Violence Seminar • Voter Registration • Global Poverty • Pink Goes Red • Family Fun Day • Breast Cancer Walk • Jazz Brunch • Buckle Up • Project Hope • AKArdid Exchange • Social Justice • PIMS • Children's Closet • Adopt a Family • Scholarships • Relay for Life • Ivy Reading AKAdemy • Financial Literacy • Salute to African American Men • Connections • Economic Security • Asthma Prevention Workshop • First Responders • MLK Day of Service

Current

Upsilon Delta Omega

Chapter Programs

Emerging Young Leaders Initiative

Soror Kere presents proper table etiquette to members of the EYL program.

Soror Veronica oversees the young girls as they test their new etiquette skills at Melange Café.

EYL participants quiz each other during the MLK Community Service Workshop.

Participants in Youth Financial Literacy Workshop.

Upsilon Delta Omega Chapter Approach

- MLK Day of Community Service
- Youth Financial Literacy Workshop
- Table Etiquette Training
- Social Networking

Economic Security Initiatives

UDO 2012 Scholarship Recipients

AKArd Exchange 2010

Sorors Dujuana and Kamala conduct
Youth Financial Education Workshop

Financial Workshop Presentation

UDO hosts Financial Workshop with
Randy Noel from State Farm.

Scholarship Recipients (above) and UDO
Members at Luncheon (below)

Upsilon Delta Omega Chapter Approach

- Annual Yuletide Jazz Brunch
- Annual Scholarship Luncheon for Award Recipients
- Economic Smart Fair

Global Poverty Initiative

Sorors Dujuana, Angela and Asha prepare to serve meals during Family Fun Day at Women's Shelter.

Sorors Jillian, Tina and Pat present children with backpacks and school supplies at the shelter.

UDO members, children and families enjoy food, music and activities at shelter cookout.

Local family receives a holiday food basket from Upsilon Delta Omega Chapter.

Upsilon Delta Omega Chapter Approach

- **Family Fun Day at Women's Shelter in Camden, NJ**
- **Adopt-A-Family Program**
- **Mothers' and Fathers' Day Baskets**

Health Initiatives

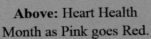

UDO Family and Friends American Cancer Society Making Strides Against Breast Cancer Walk

Above: Heart Health Month as Pink goes Red.

Right: UDO American Girls model to support the Ronald McDonald House.

UDO Members at American Cancer Society's Relay for Life.

UDO members present a donation of various goods to Ronald McDonald House

Upsilon Delta Omega Chapter Approach

- American Cancer Society—Relay for Life and Making Strides
- Heart Health Month—Pink Goes Red Activities
- UDO "American Girls" model to support the Ronald McDonald House

Internal Leadership Training for External Service Initiative

NARC 2013 UDO Display

UDO Basilei at 2012 Boule in San Francisco, CA

UDO at NARC 2013 Gala Awards dinner

UDO Ethel Hedgeman Lyle Academy Graduate

UDO Basilei at 2012 Boule in San Francisco, CA

Upsilon Delta Omega Chapter Approach

- Boule'
- NARC
- Cluster Conferences
- Leadership Conferences and Chapter Workshops
- Leadership Webinars
- Anne Mitchem Davis Officers' Institute

Social Justice and Human Rights

Legislators greeting Alpha Kappa Alpha
members at AKA Day at State House

Voter Registration at Rand Transportation
in collaboration with other Greeks

MLK Day of Service places emphasis
on Human and Civil Rights

UDO member conducts workshop on
domestic violence issues

UDO Basileus speaking at Human
Trafficking Symposium

Upsilon Delta Omega Chapter Approach

- Voter Registration Drives
- AKA Day at the State House
- Domestic Violence Workshops
- MLK Day of Service Activities

UDO Wall of Fame

Norma Evans and 26th International President and Ivy Beyond the Wall, Linda White

Shabett Harper with 31st North Atlantic Regional Director Evelyn Sample Oates

Angela Lee and 26th International Secretary Susan Simms Marsh

Gwendolyn Cobb with 31st North Atlantic Regional Director Evelyn Sample Oates

Tina Browne Sills with 28th International President Carolyn House Stewart

Claudia Brown and 32nd North Atlantic Regional Director Constance Pizarro

Shabett Harper and Patricia McGhee with 27th International President, Barbara McKinzie

UDO members with 30th North Atlantic Regional Director Joy Elaine Dailey

Gwendolyn Cobb with 27th and 26th North Atlantic Regional Directors, (l to r) Erma Barron and Ruth C. Easley

Dujuana Ambrose with 28th International President Carolyn House Stewart

UDO Wall of Fame

Norma Evans with Alicia Keys, 26th International President, Linda White and Int'l Regional Director Gloria H. Dickinson

Tina Browne Sills, Angela Lee and Gwendolyn Cobb with 23rd South Eastern Regional Director Juanita Sims Doty

Angela Lee with 28th International President, Carolyn House Stewart and 32nd North Atlantic Regional Director Constance Pizarro

Kamala Allen with Barbara Jefferson Rickett and 32nd North Atlantic Regional Director Constance Pizarro

UDO members with 28th International Secretary Susan Simms Marsh

Tina Browne Sills
with 18th International
President Dr. Mattelia B. Grays

UDO members with 28th International
Secretary Susan Simms Marsh

Angela Lee with 28th
International 1st Vice President
Dorothy Buchanan Wilson

Gwendolyn Cobb with 28th
International 1st Vice President
Dorothy Buchanan Wilson

Kameelah Majeid with 2nd
International Vice President
Shaliah Thierry

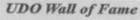

Norma Evans with Kirstin
Evans and 28th International
President Carolyn House
Stewart

Tina Browne Sills, Angela Lee and
Gwendolyn Cobb with Sonia
Sanchez

UDO Wall of Distinction

Kappa Alpha Psi Fraternity Outstanding
Achievement in Law & Government
Award winner Norma Evans

Ethel Hedgeman Lyle Leadership
Graduate Patricia McGhee

Ethel Hedgeman Lyle Leadership
Graduate Tina Browne Sills

NARC 2011 Publicity Committee

NARC 2011 Co-Chairman
Norma Evans

NARC 2011 Graphics, Signs,
Banners and Printing Committee

Education and
Scholarship Award and
National Peace Medal
Winner LaSandra
Watkins

NARC 2011 Co-Chairman, Norma
Evans with other Co-Chairmen

UDO members after chapter wins
Overall Outstanding Programs award at
NARC 2013

UPSILON DELTA OMEGA CHAPTER
"Ivies Beyond the Wall"

Bonnie Williams
Charter Member
Pecunious Grammateus

Iris A. Romantini
Charter Member
Second Anti-Basileus

Ernestine Buck
Jazz Brunch Committee

Carol Sims-Austin
Chapter Historian

Upsilon Delta Omega

Chapter Certificates

And

Awards

Alpha Kappa Alpha Sorority, Incorporated

5656 South Stony Island Avenue • Chicago, Illinois 60637-1997 • (773) 684-1282 • Fax (773) 288 8251
E-mail: normawhite@AKA1908.com

OFFICE OF THE SUPREME BASILEUS
Norma Solomon White

May 1, 1999

Upsilon Delta Omega Chapter
Alpha Kappa Alpha Sorority, Inc.,
Soror T. Faye Tucker, Basileus
24 Hazelhurst Drive
Voorhees, NJ 08043

Dear Sorors:

Indeed, it is a distinct privilege to extend GREETINGS to you as you more Upsilon Delta Omega Chapter forward in the presentation of your Fourth Annual Salute to African American Men. My heartiest and most sincere best wishes are extended for a highly successful affair. I am certain that this event will leave an excellent impression on all who share in the events of the evening.

It is my pleasure to applaud the honored recipients on this occasion for they stand far above the crowd. I know these outstanding men are being recognized for their leadership, dedication, commitment and outstanding community service. It is an honor for me to salute the recipients and commend each one of them on this auspicious occasion.

Alpha Kappa Alpha's image will, most assuredly, be raised to an even higher level in this community as you continue to provide unique experiences for youth, recognize Adrian American Men, encourage our people to "get out to vote," and focus on senior citizens, health and education. Accolades and applause to you who planned, coordinated and participated in this stellar affair. We are "BLAZING NEW TRAILS" the Alpha Kappa Alpha Way.

Sincerely,

Norma S. White
Norma Solomon White

6042 Ribault Road • Jacksonville, Florida 32209 • (904) 765-1941 • Fax (904) 765-8068
E-mail: normaaka@aol.com

STATE OF NEW JERSEY
OFFICE OF THE GOVERNOR
PO BOX 001
TRENTON
08625

CHRISTINE TODD WHITMAN
GOVERNOR

May 14, 1999

Dear Friends:

I am pleased to offer greetings to everyone attending the *Fourth Annual Salute to African American Men* sponsored by the Upsilon Delta Omega Chapter of the Alpha Kappa Alpha Sorority.

As you gather to recognize men who have distinguished themselves in community service, you celebrate the important role that African American men have long played in fostering positive change in the Garden State and throughout our nation. I join with the members of Upsilon Delta Omega Chapter and with the families, friends, and colleagues of this evening's award recipients in applauding the talents, commitment, and service that have earned for each honoree tonight's very special recognition.

My congratulations to tonight's award winners, and my best wishes to all for a memorable evening.

Sincerely yours,

Christine Whitman
Christine Todd Whitman
Governor

Alpha Kappa Alpha Sorority, Incorporated
International Standards Committee

recognizes

UPSILON DELTA OMEGA

Upon completion of the annual chapter assessment which enables the chapter
to achieve greater heights of success in sorority operations

Soror Norma S. White
Supreme Basileus

Soror Yvonne Perkins
International Standards Committee

Soror Irma Ingram
Regional Standards Committee

March 2000

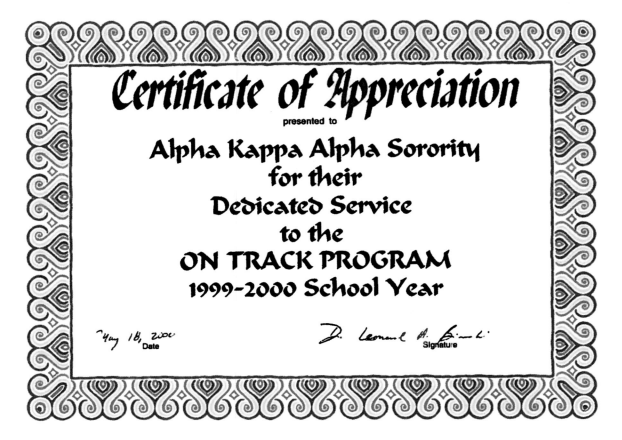

Certificate of Appreciation

presented to

Alpha Kappa Alpha Sorority
for their
Dedicated Service
to the
ON TRACK PROGRAM
1999-2000 School Year

May 18, 2000
Date

Dr. Leonard A. _____
Signature

STATE OF NEW JERSEY
OFFICE OF THE GOVERNOR
PO BOX 001
TRENTON
08695

CHRISTINE TODD WHITMAN
GOVERNOR

May 20, 2000

Dear Friends:

I am delighted to offer warm greetings to everyone attending the *Fifth Annual Salute to African American Men* sponsored by the Upsilon Delta Omega Chapter of the Alpha Kappa Alpha Sorority.

With all who appreciate the important role that African American men have long played in fostering positive change in New Jersey and throughout our nation, I salute the distinguished men being honored tonight. I join with the members of the Upsilon Delta Omega Chapter and with the families, friends, and colleagues of this evening's award recipients in applauding the contributions made by these men to the African American community and to the Garden State.

My congratulations to this year's honorees, and my best wishes to all for a memorable celebration.

Sincerely yours,

Christine Todd Whitman
Governor

Upsilon Delta Omega Chapter - 2nd Place

Chapter of the Year Award - 2001

Alpha Kappa Alpha Sorority, Incorporated

National Membership Committee

AKA is Alive in Me!

Presented to

_____

Workshop Training Module

Making Membership Work for Me!

Presented this 11th day of April, 2003

Alana M. Broady
National Membership Chairman

Joy Elaine Daley
North Atlantic Regional Director

Lamyra D. Clarke-White
North Atlantic Regional Committee Chairman

Upsilon Delta Omega Chapter Exhibit Award - 2004

Alpha Kappa Alpha Sorority, Incorporated

5656 South Stony Island Avenue • Chicago, Illinois 60637-1997 • (773) 684-1282 • Fax (773) 288-8251

Linda M. White
NATIONAL PRESIDENT

May 23, 2004

Dear Sorors of Upsilon Delta Omega:

It is with great joy that I congratulate you on the occasion of your "Salute to African American Men." This is a grand opportunity to recognize the distinguished service of exceptional black men for service, dedication and commitment to the community. Through commitment and courage your honorees have given tirelessly of themselves to improve the quality of life of others. They deserve your accolades.

My congratulations to you for the awesome presence you have established in the Cherry Hill community. Best wishes for a fabulous affair.

Sisterly,

Linda M. White

Linda Marie White

Alpha Kappa Alpha Sorority, Incorporated
North Atlantic Regional Awards Committee

A CERTIFICATE OF APPRECIATION

For your participation in the North Atlantic Regional Awards Process

To

Upsilon Delta Omega

74TH NORTH ATLANTIC REGIONAL CONFERENCE
~ Alpha Kappa Alpha on Broadway in the Spirit of Yesteryear ~
NEW YORK, NY
MARCH 17 - 20, 2005

Soror Joy Elaine Daley
North Atlantic Regional Director

Soror Cheryl Anderson Pegues
Chairman, Awards Committee

Alpha Kappa Alpha Sorority, Inc.

recognizes

Upsilon Delta Omega Chapter

for

"Building A Better Chapter"

through excellence in

Standards Reporting

75th North Atlantic Regional Conference
Atlantic City, New Jersey
March 30- April 2, 2006

Soror Joy Elaine Daley
North Atlantic
Regional Director

Soror DeVera Y. Redmond
National Standards
Committee Chairman

Soror Cheryl Petty Garnette
North Atlantic Region
Standards Committee Chairman

Alpha Kappa Alpha Sorority, Incorporated

NORTH ATLANTIC REGION

CERTIFICATE OF APPRECIATION

PRESENTED TO

Upsilon Delta Omega Chapter

CHAPTER

FOR THE *Successful Implementation* OF THE

National Connection Program

MARCH 31, 2006

NORTH ATLANTIC REGIONAL DIRECTOR

REGIONAL REPRESENTATIVE TO THE
NATIONAL CONNECTION COMMITTEE

STATE OF NEW JERSEY
OFFICE OF THE GOVERNOR
P.O. Box 001
Trenton
08625
(609) 292-6000

JON S. CORZINE
Governor

May 7, 2006

Dear Friends,

It is my pleasure to extend warm greetings to the Upsilon Delta Omega Chapter of Alpha Kappa Alpha Sorority, and everyone gathered for the 8th Salute to African American Men Awards Banquet.

New Jersey is unique in its rich ethnic diversity – some say it is our greatest strength. Our African American residents are vital parts of the cultural and economic fabric of the Garden State. This event serves as an opportunity to celebrate the positive role African American men play as contributors to our families and communities.

Best wishes for a most joyous and memorable celebration. It is only through the concern and commitment of individuals such as yourselves that we may hope to build a new and brighter future for all residents of New Jersey.

Sincerely,

Alpha Kappa Alpha Sorority, Incorporated

Centennial Membership Certificate of Award
Presented to

Upsilon Delta Omega Chapter

For their Reclamation Accomplishments of
10% Reactivation and 85% Retention
Membership Reactivation Activities

_____
Soror Evelyn Sample-Oates
North Atlantic Regional Director

Soror Constance Pizarro
Regional Membership Chairman

There's a Heart in the House of AKA

Alpha Kappa Alpha Sorority, Inc.,
North Atlantic Regional

Connection Committee
Presents

AKA Day at the Capitol
certificate of participation
Upsilon Delta Omega
Chapter

Monday, June 9, 2008
New Jersey State Capitol
Rooms 101-103, Annex
Capitol Complex
Trenton, New Jersey

Adrianne Harrison-Surgeon
Adrianne Harrison-Surgeon
NAR Connection Committee
Regional Representative

Alpha Kappa Alpha Sorority, Incorporated: 1908-2008: Celebrating 100 Years of Service to All Mankind

CERTIFICATE OF PARTICIPATION

This certificate is awarded *to*

UPSILON DELTA OMEGA

In recognition of participation during

AKA DAY AT THE CAPITOL

Evelyn Sample-Oates Centennial North Atlantic Regional Director

Adrianne Harrison-Surgeon NAR Connection Committee Chairman

Jacqueline Jennings Chapter IV Connection Committee Chairman

Date
6-9-08
Date
6-9-08
Date

In Grateful Appreciation

To

**Tina Browne-Sills
Alpha Kappa Alpha Sorority Inc.
Upsilon Delta Omega Chapter**

For sponsoring a First Responder Service Program
at Eagle's Landing – Winslow Township High School

December 3, 2008
Camden County Chapter

American Red Cross

Dr. Thomas Tudor
Chapter Chair

Alpha Kappa Alpha Sorority, Incorporated

Membership Certificate of Achievement
Presented to

Upsilon Delta Omega Chapter

For their Reclamation Accomplishments of
10% Reactivation and 85% Retention
Membership Reactivation Activities

Evelyn Sample-Oates
North Atlantic Regional Director

Constance Pizarro
North Atlantic Regional Membership Chairman

There 's a Heart in the House of AKA

Alpha Kappa Alpha Sorority Incorporated
Alpha Kappa Alpha Corporate Office • 5656 Stony Island Avenue • Chicago, IL 60637-1997 • (713) 684-1282

Office of:
Barbara A. McKinzie
International President
301 Wysteria Drive
Olympia Fields, IL 60461

May 17, 2009

Gwendolyn T. Cobb, President
Upsilon Delta Omega Chapter
Alpha Kappa Alpha Sorority, Inc.
PO Box 3607
Cherry Hill, NJ 08034

Greetings,

Best wishes on your 9th Annual Salute to African American Men Awards Banquet, honoring those individuals serving as mentors to our young Black Men. I congratulate your efforts to acknowledge their contributions and dedication to your local community. Special thanks for continuing this tradition and advancing the sorority's commitment to the growth and support of the Black Family.

Upsilon Delta Omega Chapter is to be commended on your various community programs, especially those that encourage, mentor and focus on the development of our youth. The chapter has demonstrated its involvement through a multitude of humanitarian projects, and you can be proud of the positive impact on the community you serve.

As we move forward to our new era of commitment, let us always remember our purpose "to be of service to all mankind". Let us continue to make our mark in communities everywhere and spread the Alpha Kappa Alpha story of service.

Together, we will make a difference with *Every Soror Participating*.

Sisterly Regards,

Barbara A. McKinzie
Barbara A. McKinzie
International President

BAM:dah

STATE OF NEW JERSEY
OFFICE OF THE GOVERNOR
P.O. Box 001
TRENTON
08625
(609) 292-6000

JON S. CORZINE
GOVERNOR

May 17, 2009

Dear Friends:

It is my pleasure to extend greetings to the Upsilon Delta Omega Chapter of Alpha Kappa Alpha Sorority, Inc., and everyone gathered for the 9th *Salute to African American Men Awards Banquet.*

For over a century, the Alpha Kappa Alpha Sorority has thrived as an organization of like minded college-educated women who serve the community. These women promote sisterhood while fostering leadership opportunities, spiritual growth, and an awareness of issues that affect their fellow citizens. In promoting a style of intellectual and aesthetic evaluation, Alpha Kappa Alpha Sorority, Inc. exhorts its members to stretch themselves in all directions while holding fast to a sustaining principle of achievement.

Congratulations are in order for tonight's honorees: **David Burgess, Virgil Carmen, Darryl T. Curtis, Derek Davis, Chad D. King, Marc Warren, Benjamin White, Jr., and Navarro Wright.** Alpha Kappa Alpha distinguishes these men for their generous example of leadership in dedicating their time, talents, and energy towards the betterment of future generations. In addition, I would like to join in recognizing **Tyrus Ballard, Sean Brown, Jalen Marshall, Calvin D. Evans, Jr., and Chad William King.** The Sorority has noted their many achievements and potential in becoming the leaders of tomorrow

Best wishes for an enjoyable and memorable event.

Sincerely,

JON S. CORZINE

STATE OF NEW JERSEY
OFFICE OF THE GOVERNOR
P O BOX 001
TRENTON
08625
(609) 292-6000

CHRIS CHRISTIE
GOVERNOR

June 10, 2012

Dear Friends:

On behalf of the State of New Jersey, I am pleased to extend greetings to everyone gathered for the 10th Salute to African American Men Awards Banquet hosted by the Upsilon Delta Omega Chapter of Alpha Kappa Alpha Sorority.

The service and fellowship provided by New Jersey's Greek organizations contributes greatly to the success and prosperity of our communities. The members of Upsilon Delta Omega Chapter have demonstrated a steadfast commitment to furthering AKA's mission of promoting equal opportunities for all and upholding high ethical and academic standards for college women everywhere. Through their active involvement in community programs, the Chapter's members have strived to make a positive difference in the lives of others.

For ten years, the Chapter has used this event to honor African American men whose outstanding service endeavors, academic excellence and professional accomplishments have distinguished them as role models among their peers and colleagues. I offer my congratulations to all of the individuals receiving awards today. The example they have set should serve as inspiration to everyone.

Best wishes to all for an enjoyable and memorable event.

Sincerely,

Chris Christie
Governor

Upsilon Delta Omega Chapter 2013

Overall Outstanding Program Award

94

UPSILON DELTA OMEGA TIMELESS HISTORY BIBLIOGRAPHY

Upsilon Delta Omega Chapter "Panel in Mt. Laurel sounds fresh warning over human trafficking"
Courier Post / A Gannett Company; November 3, 2013 (Andy McNeil)

Alpha Kappa Alpha Sorority, Inc. *North Atlantic Regional History 1986-1998,* 3rd History Book, Wilma
Holmes Tootle, Regional Director, Sylvia Evans Culvert, Epsilon Pi Omega, Chairwoman, NA Region
History Book Committee.

Upsilon Delta Omega Chapter. "An Exclusive International Women's Day Event With Upsilon Delta Omega,"
Ivy Leaf, Vol. 88, No. 3, Fall 2009: 74.

Upsilon Delta Omega Chapter. "Upsilon Delta Omega Aids Injured Rising Star," *Ivy Leaf,* Vol. 82, No. 2,
Summer 2001: 21

Upsilon Delta Omega Chapter. "Upsilon Delta Omega Holds AKA Alarm Project," "Upsilon Delta Omega
Holds AKA Children's Clothes Closet," "Upsilon Delta Omega Hosts its 13th Annual Yuletide Jazz
Brunch," Upsilon Delta Omega MLK Day of Service," "Upsilon Kicks Off its Ivy Reading AKAdemy,
Ivy Leaf, Vol. 85, No. 2, Summer 2006: 48-49.

Upsilon Delta Omega Chapter. "Upsilon Delta Omega Holds Annual Yuletide Brunch," *Ivy Leaf,* Vol. 88, No.
2, Summer 2009: 68.

Upsilon Delta Omega Chapter. "Upsilon Delta Omega Holds Family Fun Day," *Ivy Leaf,* Vol. 89, No. 4, Winter
2010: 54.

Upsilon Delta Omega Chapter. "Upsilon Delta Omega Honors Scholarship Recipients," *Ivy Leaf,* Vol. 87, No.
3, Fall 2008: 81-82

Upsilon Delta Omega Chapter. "Upsilon Delta Omega Hosts Seat Belt Education Poster/Essay Contest," *Ivy
Leaf,* Vol. 81, No. 2, Summer 2002: 26.

Upsilon Delta Omega Chapter. "Upsilon Delta Omega Hosts 17th Annual Yuletide Jazz Brunch," *Ivy Leaf,* Vol.
89, No. 1, Spring 2010: 59.

Upsilon Delta Omega Chapter. "Upsilon Delta Omega Launches Pilot Reading Program," *Ivy Leaf,* Vol. 82, No.
4, Winter 2003: 72.

Upsilon Delta Omega Chapter. "Upsilon Delta Omega's Martin Luther King, Jr. Day of Service," *Ivy Leaf,* Vol.
89, No. 2, Summer 2010: 88.

Upsilon Delta Omega Chapter. "Upsilon Delta Omega Presents Social Justice and Human Rights Workshop," Ivy *Leaf*, Vol. 91, No. 2, Summer 2012: 44.

Upsilon Delta Omega Chapter. "Upsilon Delta Omega Salutes African-American Men". *Ivy Leaf*, Vol. 81, No 4, Winter 2002: 28.

Upsilon Delta Omega Chapter. "Upsilon Delta Omega Salutes African-American Men," *Ivy Leaf*, Vol. 83, No. 4, Winter 2004: 53.

Upsilon Delta Omega Chapter. "Upsilon Delta Omega Sponsors AKA Children's Closet," *Ivy Leaf*, Vol. 83, No. 1, Spring 2004: 16.

Upsilon Delta Omega Chapter. "Upsilon Delta Omega Sponsors Voter Drive," *Ivy Leaf*, Vol. 88, No. 1, Spring 2009: 73.

Upsilon Delta Omega Chapter. "Upsilon Delta Omega and S.T.A.R.S. Foundation Present 18th Annual Jazz Brunch," *Ivy Leaf*, Vol. 81, No. 2, Spring 2011: 54.

Upsilon Delta Omega Chapter. "Theta Pi Omega Holds Health & Economic Smart Fair," *Ivy Leaf*, Vol. 88, No. 4, Winter 2009: 92.

Upsilon Delta Omega Chapter. "Upsilon Delta Omega Salutes African-American Men," *Ivy Leaf*, Vol. 78, No. 3, Fall 1999: 30.

Upsilon Delta Omega Chapter. "Upsilon Delta Omega Holds Annual Retreat," *Ivy Leaf*, Vol. 79, No. 3, Fall 2000: 57.

Upsilon Delta Omega Chapter. "Evans Receives Outstanding Public Official Award," *Ivy Leaf*, Vol. 82, No. 2, Summer 2003: 70.

Upsilon Delta Omega Chapter. "Upsilon Delta Omega Chartered in North Atlantic Region," *Ivy Leaf*, Vol. 73, No. 1, Spring 1995: 57.

Printed in the United States
By Bookmasters